DURAN

DURAN

DURAN DURAN

Toby Goldstein

A **2M** Communications
Production

BALLANTINE BOOKS • NEW YORK

Library of Congress Catalog Card Number: 84-90912

ISBN 0-345-32177-4

Manufactured in the United States of America

First Edition: October 1984

Cover Photos by Justin Thomas
Interior book design by Michaelis/Carpelis Design

*To Don, for his love and constant
encouragement*

CONTENTS

ACKNOWLEDGMENTS

For invaluable research help: Robin Katz in London and her counterparts in New York.

Thanks to Julie Steigman and Ebet Roberts for supplementing my observations of Duranmania with scenes they witnessed.

To *Creem* magazine, for whom I originally interviewed Duran Duran.

And to Duran Duran, who've proven that in this ridiculously complex society, it's possible to bring joy through simple entertainment and not feel guilty about it.

ECSTASY

A strange and wonderful tension was filling the air inside New York City's Madison Square Garden, as small groups of the 20,060 ticket holders for the first of Duran Duran's two sold out shows strolled, ran, and bounded to their seats. Long lines of customers parted with hard-earned salaries or saved-up allowance money to buy colorful concert programs, elegantly designed 1984 tour T-shirts, and other souvenirs of the one show they'd never want to forget. As the youngest fans impatiently waited for the night to begin, their squeals of tightly-held-in ecstasy gave life to the Garden's expanse of grimy gray concrete.

Backstage, as opening act Prince Charles and the City Beat Band valiantly struggled to hold the attention of the charged-up, over-excited crowd, a different kind of tension was taking place. Simon Le Bon played the video game Fighter Pilot and yelled out the scores he racked up, to his father John's dismay. Simon had been having minor throat problems on this tour, and no one wanted anything to jeopardize this all-important show. Other parents—except for Andy Taylor's father, the only one not present tonight—quietly chatted with their sons. When the boys disappeared to change into their stage clothes and makeup, their families shared a couple of beers and sang English pub songs—all friends despite several very different backgrounds.

3

The between-set break seemed to last for hours, though it was only about thirty minutes long. Finally, a video cameraman appeared onstage, making final adjustments to ensure that the simultaneous on-screen projection of the show would happen smoothly. Down came the familiar red-and-white backdrop reading "Coca-Cola"—sponsors of the entire tour. Then, accompanied by a torrent of shrieks and screams, the number 7 and a tiger face—symbols of the *Seven and the Ragged Tiger* LP, flashed on the screen. Like one person, the audience leapt up from the edges of their plastic seats and stood tip-toe on the chairs, determined not to miss one minute of the ninety-minute set. Equally determined to make this show—their Madison Square Garden debut—live up to all the hopes they had for such a night, Duran Duran: Simon Le Bon, Nick Rhodes, Andy Taylor, John Taylor, and Roger Taylor, ran up the backstage ramp and onto the majestic-sized stage, undisputed rulers of all they surveyed.

In a harmony of style and attitude, the most devout fans, who called themselves Durannies, matched the carefree glamour of their heroes. Simon's well-crafted workout gear and Nick's graceful silks were copied by hundreds of girls, some with dates whose sartorial splendor rivaled that of the band. Wristbands, scarves, bits of leather, and sashes draped many a slender, bouncing body as each person whirled and danced to the music, in his or her own private space. Some fans had created and draped giant signs over balconies with impossible to ignore messages like "A Kiss for Duran Duran" or "Roger—Take Me Away!" Others, unable to resist the hypnotic music that called to them as the band played its first song, "Is There Something I Should Know?", flung themselves at the stage, tossing gifts of clothing, stuffed animals, and a sea of notes with telephone numbers at their favorite group member.

Smiling with the unblemished joy of achieving what many had judged impossible, Duran Duran shared their happiness at being here with the audience in a parade of hits. The opener was followed by "Hungry Like the Wolf," "The Reflex," "New Moon on Monday," and "Union of the Snake," a sequence that had the audience edging into the aisles to dance. After the chart topper-filled introduction, the band weaved in a group of ballads and lesser known album tracks throughout the show, a standout being the tender "Save a Prayer."

By adding four guest musicians to the lineup, the group were able to closely reproduce their full-bodied recordings onstage, and bring the show to a walloping finale with old favorites "Planet Earth" and "Careless Memories." Of course, that wasn't enough for the crazed crowd, who summoned them back for encores of "Rio" and "Girls on Film." Then, as magically as the show had begun, it was over. The audience, clutching their souvenirs and their memories, slowly trickled out of the reverberating hall. Reliving favorite moments and especially breathtaking images with a friend or two, they headed for home.

And backstage, too, the physical demands of entertaining a huge audience were giving way to a different kind of happiness among the band, their families, and friends. They were relieved that the show had gone so well without a hitch. They were proud that their Madison Square Garden debut, which had sold out in just three hours, lived up to the expectations of their fans, as well as their own. But most of all, Duran Duran were filled with a kind of awe—that, less than five years after this band had begun to drift together in Birmingham, England; less than three years after their first album, *Duran Duran*, was released in America— only to disappear from sight because it was widely ignored on radio; that after overcoming obstacles resulting from being categorized as one thing, then meanly put down for being something else—THEY HAD DONE IT. Duran Duran had sold out two shows at Madison Square Garden, a place they had dreamed of playing as the ultimate symbol of a band's success.

Less than a year earlier, John Taylor had predicted

to a dubious reporter that Duran Duran had a master plan, which included scaling the heights of Madison Square Garden by 1984. Now, Andy Taylor could look back at his success and proudly tell a journalist from *Melody Maker* who was touring with the group, "It's *the* dream. It's the dream you have when you're a kid. I think it's the most prestigious gig in the world—everyone's played there who's ever existed. I read about it in Ian Hunter's *Diary of a Rock'n'Roll Star* when I was eleven, and I've wanted to play there for the last twelve years." Or, as Simon Le Bon enthused, "Madison Square Garden is a very special place as far as music is concerned. There has always been history made there. Playing there, for us, is almost like doing a very exclusive gig."

Such an accomplishment is worthy of praise for any performer who can do it. But in the hard-to-please world of rock and roll, there aren't that many performers who successfully scale its highest peaks. And it's been a very long time since a group of musicians aged twenty-one to twenty-five—not even a decade older than many of their most devout followers—have racked up those kind of praises. From anonymity to world fame, from being ignored as starstruck kids with dreams to talented artists living those dreams, from Birmingham England's industrial landscape as their backyard to all of planet Earth as their playground, Duran Duran's journey to superstardom reflects the power of positive thinking at its most persuasive. Wishing was the first step, making the wishes come true the steps that followed and still lead upward. . . .

THE EARLY YEARS

*S*how business was a tradition in the Le Bon family, but it had bypassed a generation when Simon John Charles Le Bon was born on October 27, 1958—sharing his birthday with his father, John. The robust, 7 lb., 12 oz. boy first saw the light of day in Bushey Maternity Hospital near Watford, a pleasant suburb just northwest of London. Simon's grandmother had enjoyed a career as one of the Tiller Girls during the early 1900s, and his mother's aunt once danced before the Queen with the famous Ziegfeld Follies. However, Simon's mother Ann had curtailed her own performing aspirations to raise her eldest son and his two brothers, Jonathan and David, while the boys' father pursued a successful career as a London Water Board executive.

According to Mrs. Le Bon, Simon was a sensitive and imaginative child from the start, spouting his own little poems at the age of two and a half. Determined not to let the boy's budding talents go to waste, she enrolled Simon in twice-a-week after-school acting classes from age five. It wasn't long before the blond-haired, blue-eyed charmer landed the first of several television commercials, appearing as the boy with the "dirty" shirt in a detergent ad. That Persil detergent spot was followed by soft drink, coffee and magazine commercials on TV, eventually leading young Simon to the stage. By age fourteen, he had performed in various amateur productions, starting with *The King and I* at seven, and making his debut in the West End (London's equivalent to Broadway) in the musical, "Tom Brown's Schooldays." For Simon, being written about and photographed in his neighborhood newspapers had become just another acknowledgment of his developing skills—an appealing indication of all the photos and interviews to come.

Ann Le Bon remembers that Simon's academic talents took a definite back seat to his performing interests. Though far from unintelligent, Simon was an average student at the West Lodge Junior School and Pinner Grammar School (the latter attended years earlier by another suburbanite destined for worldwide acclaim—Reg Dwight a/k/a Elton John). Mrs. Le Bon was told by Simon's teachers that the boy preferred dreaming of ideas to actually writing them down. Another instructor, recognizing what would shortly become obvious, opined that if Simon were only taught music, art, and drama, his grades would be admirable. It also seems that Simon possessed another not-so-admirable quality—procrastination. His mother observed to an English magazine, "Simon always did his homework at the last minute. I left it entirely up to him. He was very reasonable. He knew that if he hadn't done it, he hadn't done it. I never chased him because he always had so much to do.

"But he had to try and fit in because he realized he needed some academic qualifications. He didn't want to be a one-sided person." If he didn't turn his reports in on time, Simon didn't neglect his own thoughts. He spent a lot of time composing fanciful tales, sprawled on the living room carpet, and had several poems, drawings, and stories published in the school magazines *Quill* and *Pinnacle*. And despite preferring to put his imagination to work instead of plodding through assignments, Simon did leave Grammar School with six 'O' levels (ordinary passes) and two 'A' levels (advanced passes), in Art and English.

After refusing to stick with the Boy Scouts (claiming that the other youths kicked him at his first meeting!), Le Bon joined the local church choir, St. John's, and was encouraged by the church organist, Mr. Turvey. Under the man's tutelage, Simon enjoyed choir practice and attended church twice during the week and twice on Sundays. In fact, it was through the choir that Simon, at age thirteen, made his very first recording— though it was never publicly released. A local company recorded Simon singing the hymn "He Shall Feed His Flock," with Mr. Turvey's accompaniment. No one would doubt that Le Bon's patiently trained soprano voice held a genuine gift, and when he began to mature, Mrs. Le Bon ensured that Simon would protect it. He followed her advice and quit the choir as soon as his voice started cracking, then learned from his own operatically trained mother the proper way to sing.

Yet Simon then moved in a direction quite unlike the one his family had envisioned. By 1977, he'd drifted through a brief stay at art school, left a printing apprenticeship unfinished, and discovered that he looked terrific with a tan during a working holiday at an Israeli kibbutz. Simon really enjoyed that job, he recalled. "I drove a tractor, did lumberjacking and orange picking, and looking after kids. It's very hot in Israel. So, you get up at the crack of dawn or earlier and work for four hours a day. By lunchtime it's too hot to do anything but rest. So I'd work in the morning, then swim and sunbathe, and see my girlfriends later in the afternoon. It was a very healthy lifestyle."

When he came back home, the English music scene was solidly in the black-leathered grip of punk, and Simon joined the fray by forming his own punk rock band called Dog Days. Le Bon fondly remembered the group as surviving many rehearsals but only one actual gig, at the Harrow Technical College 1978 End of Summer term dance. They were the opening act, had to play on the floor, and because they went on too long, the plugs were pulled—right in the middle of Le Bon's vocals. Somehow, Simon realized, there had to be a better way of doing things.

Attempting to further his education, Simon took a day job as a hospital porter and studied for an additional 'A' level at night. In 1979, he applied to study drama at Birmingham University and was accepted. While at school, Simon dated a girl named Fiona Kemp. He got through that first (and only) year of college, but by the summer of 1980, felt that creative urge bubbling to the surface again. Simon Le Bon needed a way to channel his energies and Fiona, who worked as a barmaid in Birmingham's hippest club, the Rum Runner, thought she might have the answer. Some friends of hers who called themselves Duran Duran were looking for a singer, and Simon decided to audition. He figured that at least it might be an interesting way to get through the summer. Showing up for his tryout in sunglasses and a punky pair of pink spotted leopard-skin trousers, Simon Le Bon presented the fledgling group with an image they couldn't ignore. And when they tried out a few songs together, the band knew that here was the missing link to forge a chain of success. Now, realized Nick Rhodes and John Taylor, the cause to which they'd dedicated their lives for almost two years stood a fair chance of paying off.

If Duran Duran has a founding father, bass player John Taylor is that man. It was he who started the group in 1978, when he was barely eighteen, naming it after a character in the early 1960s sci-fi film "Barbarella." (Jane Fonda acted in the leading role.)

John Taylor's parents, Jean and Jack Taylor, still live in the semi-detached Birmingham house where they raised their son, ironically, in a section of the town called Hollywood. The offspring of a car components worker (now retired) and a children's school teacher, Nigel John Taylor was born on June 20, 1960, at Sorrento Hospital in Birmingham, weighing a healthy 6 lbs., 13 oz. The blond-haired brown-eyed boy was always the apple of his parents' eyes, and to this day, considers the modest family home his own, though he rarely gets to spend more than a few days on each visit. John's small but well-loved room is where he used to let his vivid imagination run wild. In its security, he practiced dance steps, trying to overcome a persistent shyness about dancing in public, and of course, he spent hours tucked away listening to music.

John's mother, Jean, remembers how, almost from the first, her son favored the creative fields over his regular schoolwork. He attended Our Lady of the Wayside Junior School, Redditch Grammar School, and completed his formal education with a twelve-month design course at Birmingham Polytechnic. "He was always very good at art," said Mrs. Taylor. "He got five 'O' levels and an 'A' level in art. He really didn't have that much homework to do. He spent a great deal of time painting toy soldiers. It was a very complicated and skilled job. He was really enthusiastic and we used to take him to exhibitions all over the country. Then, suddenly, he went right off it. We still have his collection, though."

John's teachers also observed that, although their pupil was an eager learner and didn't hesitate to pipe up in classroom discussions, the youth left much to be desired in his written work. His good grades in reading, spelling, and, of course, art were undercut by poor marks in arithmetic and physical activities. John has always been lean, strong and agile, but he didn't share the typical young British boy's interest in sports.

By the age of fourteen, John was getting more inspired reading weekly pop music papers such as the *New Musical Express*, or dreaming about the fine cars he wanted to own, than devoting hours to schoolwork. "I'd be sitting there looking at logarithms and I'd think, well, what's the point of this? I wish they'd teach me to drive instead," John recalled, years later. Mrs. Taylor also remembers how much her son had a passion for fine cars, and vowed that one day he'd be able to buy any model he fancied. Now, when John's busy with any of Duran Duran's many projects, his father takes expert care of Taylor's beautiful, luxurious Aston Martin.

Growing steadily more impatient with traditional school obligations, John asked one of his teachers for guitar lessons. The instrument wasn't serious enough to be taught in school, he was told. From that moment on, John knew that any advancement in making the music he loved could only come from his own initiative. John curtly turned down the music teacher's hint that he concentrate on a proper orchestral instrument. When a compromise suggestion to learn saxophone was also refused, Taylor began an intense period of self-instruction. He now regrets not taking advantage of piano lessons offered by the school, but feels that academia held little else for him.

John started out as a guitar player—and in fact played guitar and bass on the very first Duran Duran demo tape—but eventually concentrated on the rhythm instrument. "There's not a lot that I feel I can technically accomplish that I want to." He candidly admitted that he's never been interested in playing a really great bass. "It would be quite nice, I suppose, but it doesn't bother me. I've always been more interested in the color of the trousers, really."

John's devotion to pop music rapidly grew into an obsession, and his mother remembers her son always rushing off to see other bands. By the time he was in his middle teens, Taylor had dropped the "Nigel" from his name—it's just not a very cool sounding name in Britain, kind of like Herbert or Irving is in the United States—and as plain old John, began his year at art college. That was to be a very important year for him when he formed the original incarnation of Duran Duran with a college chum, Steve Duffy, a clarinetist, Simon Colley, and John's longtime friend, keyboardist Nick Rhodes.

In fact, in the beginning, Duran Duran had a much stronger visual identity than it did a musical one. John used the posters he'd designed for his newly hatched group as college art projects, concentrating on the only three colors he enjoyed using at the time—red, black, and white. For a while, Taylor made an effort to play by the college's rules, but soon found himself again chaffing at academic restrictions. While his first-term exhibition of the posters won high marks, John's final presentation for term end, of the first Duran demo tape, was nowhere near what the school desired of its students. "I suppose I was testing them up to a point," John admitted to writer Kasper de Graaf, "because art college teachers think they're progressive. But when you say to them, 'Look, I've created this out of nothing; isn't this the same as writing on paper?' they don't quite know how to handle it." John received his college pass more out of nerve than a performance up to standards. Taylor knew, from then on, that he and Nick were doing the right thing, the only thing they could, and no matter how long it might take until they became headliners in the music press, their efforts were worth the struggle.

When Nick Rhodes' handwriting was analyzed recently, it revealed quite a lot about the stylish synthesizer player, and why his contributions to Duran Duran have always been so inspired. Nick is independent, ambitious, and single-minded. But he can also be moody, restless, and show his ego in public. He likes to have his own way, but finds it difficult to fit in because of a constant urge to start new projects. Rhodes understands how other people are motivated, and if he chooses to, can share many inventive ideas with his friends. The analyst reported that Nick's first impressions are always likely to be the best for him. And Nick has been the kind of person who's listened to his instincts, even when they often led him down an unconventional path.

Born on June 8, 1962, in Mosely, Nicholas James Bates was raised in Birmingham by his parents, Sylvia, a former toy shop owner, and Roger, an engineer—just a mile or so away from John Taylor. Years later, Nick said goodbye to "Bates" and hello to "Rhodes" because his real name seemed too ordinary, and "Rhodes" conjured up tantalizing images of the classic Fender Rhodes keyboard.

To put it mildly, Nick and schoolwork didn't get along. By nature an observer of life, Rhodes preferred watching other students in class to completing his own projects. He once described his first day of school as a nightmarish experience in which, "I had to sit down and listen to this rather tall, skinny—almost ugly—screaming dragon teach a bunch of idiots and me to read and write." He wasn't stupid, of course, just impatient, and soon realized that he could either follow the rules and learn to pass exams—or, he could adapt the classroom to his own use, as a laboratory for observing how people behaved. Wisely or not, Nick concentrated on learning real-life psychology and let his exams fall by the wayside.

"I left school as soon as I could, at sixteen," Nick said, unashamedly. "I got my 'O' levels and ran. School really stifled me. I really didn't feel that I needed to know what sodium bicarbonate and sulphuric acid make." Instead, Rhodes planned to become worthy of the name he'd chosen for himself. Totally self-taught, he began by groping out two-finger melodies on a cheap WASP synthesizer. Obviously, Nick had a natural talent for music, progressing from those humble beginnings to mastering record productions for other talents. And from the first, Rhodes played a major part in shaping Duran Duran's songs.

Unlike the widely traveled Le Bon, or even his long-time Birmingham chum John Taylor, Nick never had any ambitions towards "normal" work. Immediately after leaving school, Rhodes became a disc jockey in Birmingham's top club, the Rum Runner. Just as he used to observe people in the classroom, Nick would pick records for the ceaselessly churning crowds on the dance floor, but never went out there himself. His detailed cataloging of people has made for some bizarre experiences. After Duran Duran had visited America a few times, Nick and Simon went to a radio station in a New York suburb. Upon returning from the visit, Rhodes imitated the accents of the men who'd driven them to and from the station—with perfect New York slang and huge chunks of the conversations he had tucked into his memory.

Even before he had a name for the group of his dreams, John Taylor enlisted Nick Rhodes into the band. The twosome often hung out at the Rum Runner—a club as important to Duran Duran as the Cavern was to the Beatles—planned strategy, and wrote songs. At that time, punk rock was the major driving force in English music, but it didn't appeal to Nick or John. They preferred the studied elegance of Roxy Music's lead singer Bryan Ferry, master innovator David Bowie, and Rod Stewart—then halfway to self-imposed exile in America and already a major superstar. "Within the band there are really only two unanimous influences," Nick revealed, "and those are Roxy Music and the Beatles. The former, because of their sophisticated approach, and the latter because they wrote great pop melodies." As an example of the song form he admires, Nick brought up one of the earliest Duran Duran tracks, "Girls on Film," in an interview with *Melody Maker*.

"It's so obvious, really, that the simplest things in the end are always the best. A good pop song is something you can whistle, and you can only whistle one note at a time. So if it's ridiculously complicated, you

can't do it. If it goes, 'girls on film...girls on film,'
it's easy to whistle, it's one note, I can play it with
one finger. In fact," he joked, "that's my little test. I
have to be able to play everything with one finger. If
it's two fingers, it's too complicated."

In addition to John and Nick, the first group included Steve Duffy on vocals and occasionally on bass,
and Simon Colley, who played bass and clarinet. The
group, which was almost called RAF—the letters do
not stand for Royal Air Force, or anything else—had
just been named by John. Nick remembers the day he
and Taylor were enjoying some beers at a pub called
the Hole in the Wall and John came up with Duran
Duran. What a relief! thought Rhodes, who was fed
up with poring over books and film titles, and wanted
a name that he could live with.

In the summer of 1978, Duran Duran phase I de-
buted in another of Birmingham's hip clubs, Barbarella's, supporting an equally early lineup of art rockers,
Fashion. People who heard those early dates remember
the group sounding a little like Soft Cell. That, however, was destined to evolve as Colley and Duffy quit—
Simon to head off in a more straightforward rock and
roll direction, and Steve to become a novelist. (Though
Duffy has not yet achieved fame as an author, he did
release a single last year under the name TinTin: "Hold
It"/"Blowing Kisses.")

To repopulate the group, Nick and John took a look
around the local pop scene, and next recruited vocalist
Andy Wickett, who'd been performing with a New
York Dolls-influenced band called TV Eye. Since the
Dolls had always been about image, Rhodes and Taylor
hoped Andy would do; and for his part, Wickett wanted
to play with a more "conceptual" outfit. By this time,
Nick's rhythm box was proving both limited and un-
reliable for percussion. It was a lucky night when Andy
Wickett went to a party and invited drummer Roger
Taylor to a Duran Duran rehearsal. Roger's rather high

level of musical skill was just what the primitive band needed. Though only a few months older than John, Roger was way ahead on his instrument.

"I've always been the quiet one. The kid who sat at the back of the class and said nothing," admitted Roger Taylor, who seems to come by his shyness quite naturally. According to Roger's mother, Jean, now a retired accounting clerk, her second son was placid, even as a baby, in contrast to his older brother Steve, now twenty-seven. Roger was born in Heathville Hospital, in the Birmingham suburb of Castle Bromwich, on April 26, 1960. Whenever he's at home, Roger still lives in his parents' house.

Born a hefty baby at 8 lbs., 9 oz, young Roger was an agreeable younger son in a family that eventually numbered six; Taylor has two younger sisters, surely among the most envied girls in the world! According to Mrs. Taylor, Roger progressed without incident through Castle Bromwich Junior School and Park Hall School, graduating with five 'O' levels. Taylor made no plans to attend a college or university, and he wasn't pressured about it, though his mother was not very thrilled when her son's fanaticism for pop music showed indications of becoming a full-time career. "Even at a young age, I can remember Roger bashing away at milk bottles with my knitting needles. It used to drive me mad! That was his first attempt at drumming. I didn't think anything of it then," she admitted.

From the age of ten, Roger loved pop music, and followed his older brother's Motown tastes. The first band Taylor went to see live was the Jackson Five. A few years later, when punk first started peeking out of basements and alleyways, Roger was heavily influenced by the progressive rock band Genesis. However, Taylor was up on current trends sufficiently that the earliest groups he played in professionally were punk bands; they had the appropriately repulsive names of Crucified Toad and the Scent Organs—the latter, a semilegendary group Roger was still part of when he was asked to join Duran Duran.

There wasn't much time or much money in Roger's life to allow him a very active social scene. As he has told the press: "I was a late bloomer. I didn't start going with girls until I was fifteen. Even then, the first date I went on consisted of going for a walk around the park in Birmingham. That's what a lot of us did. We couldn't afford to go anywhere."

Because Roger had developed a keen interest in boating and water sports at a young age, his parents were pleased that upon leaving school he went to work in a yacht shop. Eventually, Taylor bought a boat of his own. But when Roger sold the boat in order to buy his first set of drums, the Taylors were horrified. Mrs. Taylor admits trying to persuade her son from throwing his life away on false hopes. "Really, I think most parents would have done the same in our position," she said, looking back on that turbulent era. "We thought he really didn't have a chance, and never dreamed that Roger would be an international star just a few years later.

"But he was quiet and determined and once he sets his mind on something that's it, he won't move. He put the drums in his bedroom and, naturally, that caused quite a few upsets. So we set a time limit and he could only bash at them until a certain hour." By 1977, when Roger joined the Scent Organs, the Taylors were sorely strained. For a while, the group practiced in each other's homes, until pictures started flying off the Taylors' walls! Mrs. Taylor obtained permission for the band to practice at the local church hall, until the vicar had so many complaints he threw them out, too. To make matters worse, impatient with having no place to play, the Scent Organs set up a stage in the middle of the Taylors' road and put on a street concert. "A disaster," is how Mrs. Taylor described it.

Soon after their alfresco fiasco, Roger signed up

with Duran Duran, to his parents' dismay. "We used to say to Roger, 'This is ridiculous—you're going to end up with nothing.' Then he came home one night and told he me was playing his first gig with Duran Duran at a local wine bar in Birmingham, called the Hosteria. I decided to go along to see what he was up to. A couple of friends from work came along with me for support. My husband Hughie refused to go. When I came out, I couldn't believe it. I was really bowled over."

Clearly, Roger Taylor's sultry fifties-style good looks, coupled with the dance-oriented skilled drumming he brought to Duran Duran, gave them a major boost. Roger, Andy Wickett, and Nick assisted John in creating the band's rough-hewn first demo tape, which included a very early "Girls on Film." More changes would have to occur, however, before the enthusiastic teenagers obtained any serious interest in the new music they were creating, tucked away in Birmingham. The hard path they were on resulted in no win situations like one show they played at Birmingham University, where the band competed with a rough sports party. The audience started throwing paper plates and sausages at the band, and then they moved up to ashtrays and glasses. "Afterwards," said John, when all the damage was totalled, "People came up to us and said, 'It's nothing against you personally; it's just that we wanted to have a good time tonight.'"

For reasons no one in the band could figure out, Andy Wickett abruptly quit once the demo tape was completed. While the remaining threesome searched for a new singer, they steadily moved towards a more distinct Duran Duran sound, one which had a dance beat. John, who'd previously thought of himself as a "flash" guitar player, à la Mick Ronson of David Bowie's Ziggy Stardust band—started paying close attention to bass players, spurred by Roger's enthusiasm about the American group, Chic. Then, too, Roger was

the very first drummer Duran Duran had who didn't
come out of a rhythm box! The more of Taylor's controlled drumming John heard, the more he wanted to
play with him. Eventually, John shifted to bass and
the combination was a happy one all around.

Although a move in the right direction, this left Duran
Duran in need of a singer and a guitarist. They placed
an ad in a music paper desiring a "modern guitarist for
Roxy/Bowie influenced band," and took on a Lon-
doner named Alan Curtis. Singing duties would be handled by Roger's former colleague in the Scent Organs,
Jeff Thomas.

Thinking they were set for a while, this third version
of Duran Duran rehearsed a tight, R&B flavored set
in one of Birmingham's down-at-heels industrial areas.
Songs like Rod Stewart's "Do Ya Think I'm Sexy",
the Rolling Stones' "Miss You," and Giorgio Morod-
er's disco chart-toppers were among their biggest in-
spirations. Meanwhile, two of the most important music
men in Birmingham—brothers Paul and Michael Berrow, who had just bought the Rum Runner club—were
visiting New York, where the unbelievable drawing
power of discos like Studio 54 and Xenon mightily
impressed them. They returned to England and set
about transforming the Rum Runner into a similarly
chic, elite appeal nightclub.

Taken with the club's weekly "Roxy/Bowie Nights,"
Nick and John thought that the Rum Runner's new
policy might be a good place for them to find work.
The Berrows liked the four-track tape handed them
enough to offer Duran Duran rehearsal space and a
series of gigs. Eventually, the brothers realized the
group's enormous potential and, several months later,
became Duran Duran's managers.

Unfortunately for the two newish members, every
upward move exerts a price. Alan Curtis and Jeff
Thomas left the band, whether by choice or not is
uncertain. Stalwarts Nick, Roger, and John vowed to

change the haphazard way in which they'd been re-
populating their band. Now surer than ever of what
they wanted from their membership: young, aggressive
musicians sympathetic to dance rhythms of the day,
the trio auditioned dozens of singers and guitarists.
Occasionally, one or another was tried out, but no one
seemed quite right. Desperate, they again turned to the
music press and advertised for a "live-wire guitarist."
They got Andy Taylor and, despite what must have
been astonishment at the idea of a band with three
Taylors—none of them related, all knew Andy was
their man.

Andrew Taylor speaks in a dialect of English that's
almost uncomprehensible unless he speaks very, very
slowly. It betrays Taylor's northern origins, where he
was born, in Tynemouth Royal Infirmary, near Newcastle, on February 16, 1961. Unlike the other members of his prospective group, whose backgrounds were
fairly middle class, Andy belonged to a poor, hard-
working fisherman's family. His father and grandfather
both were men of the sea, and all three generations
shared a house in the tiny village of Cullercoats. His
childhood had few luxuries—the house had an outside
toilet and tin bath. As Andy grew up, a good student
who loved playing soccer, his father changed careers—
away from the declining fishing industry, becoming a
carpenter.

Relating a tale that seems too awful to be part of
Duran Duran's largely sunny history, Andy remembers
passing his exams for grammar school, going to his
new school a happy eleven-year-old, and coming home
to discover that his mother had packed up and left.
Andy's father had to raise Taylor and his younger
brother on his own. One thing he did was buy his son
an electric guitar for Christmas. "I started taking lessons from a man across the road named Dave Black,"
Andy recalled. "He was essentially a jazz player, but
he got me started at the cost of a pound a lesson."

Because of the family upheavals, the Taylors moved and Andy wound up in a school that didn't challenge his brain. By the age of thirteen, he'd all but abandoned formal education in favor of music. Andy didn't wish to become a bricklayer or plumber, as the career counselors had advised him. He wanted to play guitar.

Simply disappearing from school two years before he ought to have left, Andy played with a constantly changing series of bands, working in men's clubs up north, strip clubs on the Continent, and air bases. Taylor performed in almost six hundred gigs before he auditioned for Duran Duran, including thirteen months throughout Germany (shades of the Beatles!), ten weeks in a Greek beach club, and a difficult time in Luxembourg, Belgium, where he was held at gunpoint by the local police! Why? Simply for trying to convince a club owner to pay up the two thousand dollars he owed Taylor.

Safely back in England and yearning for a group who shared his dedication, Andy saw Duran Duran's *Melody Maker* ad and, with a phone call, arranged an audition. Selling all he owned—except his guitar and Marshall amp—for a train ticket, Andy Taylor went to Birmingham, found the Rum Runner...and came face to face with "the biggest bunch of weirdos I'd seen." Since, underneath the blue denim jeans that turned Nick right off, Andy wanted to be "weird" himself, he felt, that, given enough time to develop the right visual image, he'd fit right into Duran Duran. He did quite a selling job, Rhodes remembers, telling the group they'd fall apart if he wasn't accepted! Fortunately, Andy's playing fit so precisely into the niche John wanted filled that he was taken on right away. "People could play the Johnny Thunders rock lines but they couldn't do the Chic rhythms," John said, summing up the horde of applicants. "And we badly needed that crossover in the band." Andy Taylor easily handled both. Plus, he just happened to be a fan of Gary

Moore's guitar style—at the time, one of John Taylor's favorite axemen.

When Andy Taylor started rehearsing with Duran Duran, the group didn't want to admit they were still without a singer. Nick used to tell him that the singer went on vacation, so they were auditioning new ones. In the meantime, as the Berrows' investment in the group increased, the search intensified. Duran Duran's new managers bought John a bass guitar and Nick his first decent quality synthesizer. More than a few times, the brothers gave homeless Andy Taylor a place to sleep in their house. In return, the band all helped in running the Berrows' club; Andy painted walls, John polished mirrors, Roger worked in a factory, and Nick was the DJ. All manner of people hung out at the Rum Runner, checking each other's threads, listening to the hard-edged dance music Nick Rhodes loved to spin, catching up on the latest gossip with in-the-know barmaids like Fiona Kemp. When she became aware that the house band, Duran Duran, were in dire straits for a singer, she told her former boyfriend, Simon Le Bon, who arranged to meet Nick and Roger the very next day.

Well, at least Simon didn't want to be another Johnny Rotten, and take after the Sex Pistols' notorious snarling vocalist, the band noted with relief. If anything, Le Bon's outrageous pink trousers and his theatrical presentation were a bit too expansive and larger-than-life. "Perhaps all Simon's notes weren't in perfect pitch, but he had good ideas for lyrics, the outlook, and a great pair of leopardskin trousers," Nick Rhodes told the press. With the threesome impressed with each other's accomplishments and attitudes, Simon was asked to come back the next day to rehearse with the group. An enthusiastic Le Bon went home, wrote a song called "The Sound of Thunder" on the spot, and brought it back with him. John heard Simon sing the

lyrics and realized, "It was one of those magic moments. We were all playing, and we looked round at
each other and said, 'Yeah, this is it.'" Duran Duran
had officially begun. How far they would go, no one
even dared to dream.

POST-PUNK
RHYTHMS

*N*othing in England changes as fast as the music its young people listen to, the bands they go to see, the clubs where they dance, and especially the way they dress and style their hair. First, it was the fifties rock'n'rollers in black leather jackets, blue jeans, and pointy-toed boots. Another generation, who first heard the Beatles, the Who, the Yardbirds and their many imitators in the 1960s called themselves mods. The guys wore jackets with narrow lapels and chino slacks to match. At parties, they danced all night with their miniskirted girlfriends to the best sounds of Motown and early soul music. Of course, the psychedelic hippies came next, and it was anything goes—the wilder, the better. But if you felt like settling down to groove on Jimi Hendrix and Pink Floyd in a well-worn pair of blue denim bell bottoms, that was OK, too. Anyone who wanted to fit in, was in—as long as you were cool and "did your own thing."

This sort of anti-fashion hung on in America until very recently, and still exists among heavy metal fans. In Britain, though, blue jeans gave way to the brilliantly colored silks and satins of the "glam rockers." And they were very important to Duran Duran, who were just entering their teens as the seventies wore on. "Because of our age, we didn't really grow up with the

Rolling Stones," Nick Rhodes declared. "We grew up with Roxy Music, David Bowie, Cockney Rebel, and Sparks." Those guys were brimful of style. Bowie, then in his exotic Ziggy Stardust and Thin White Duke phases, changed his hair color every time he cut a new album. On several of Bowie's album covers, he wore makeup—not to look like a girl, but to enhance his already seductive appeal. Roxy Music's lead singer, Bryan Ferry, was another heart-throb who didn't try to hide his good looks. He sang the group's torchy love songs dressed in sharp white suits and wide-brimmed hats. They had class, and their songs were great for dancing; that pairing became an irresistible attraction for the future Durans.

Before too long, though, the glam-rock scene became too big for the clubs that started it. Groups packed up tons of equipment and hired huge road crews in order to survive through lengthy tours of America. There was a living to be made in the United States—as long as a band was willing to perform in the horrible acoustics of arenas, often to thousands of kids messed up on drugs. Requirements for a band became more demanding; if a group didn't have masses of equipment and a big-shot manager, they weren't going anywhere. Young musicians were being closed out, and they didn't like it one bit. Something had to give, and that was when punk burst onto the scene.

Considering Duran Duran's carefully designed outfits, their friendliness to audiences, and the fact that the band now plays in arenas around the world, it seems strange to imagine its members owing a huge debt to ferocious punk. But they do, and no one is uncomfortable admitting so. "Let's face it," said Simon, in an early *Melody Maker* interview, "this band wouldn't exist if it wasn't for the Sex Pistols or the Clash. They really inspired us to play." Nick commented that he was still in school when punk really took off; in 1977, he was only fifteen. While he wasn't tempted to dress like a punk, with ripped clothes and safety pins, Rhodes did go to see every band who played at Barbarella's. Some were good, he remembers, like Siouxsie and the Banshees and the Buzzcocks. Some weren't. And the best were the Sex Pistols. "I saw the Pistols a few times and I've never witnessed a band with energy like that—ever," Nick said with admiration.

The punks showed young players that it didn't take a ton of money to get gigs and attract attention. It was the most natural thing in the world for most of Duran Duran to put in their band apprenticeships with neighborhood punkers. "It opened our eyes because they were playing small clubs," Nick said. "They couldn't play that well, but they were getting on the stage and after about six months, they had a Top 30 album. So we thought, 'If they can do it, we can do it'... Before, when it was sort of Pink Floyd, Yes, and Genesis, bands like that, you never dreamed you could be in a band."

Like many of his friends, and millions of record buyers in Britain, Nick thought that punk was great. Its excitement broke all the rules that the old fashioned music-business types had set up. Punk bands really didn't care whether or not they could get booked on a big American tour. It was more important to play at home. England needed to break its dependence on America for ideas, like it had done when the Beatles first broke through, and punk was the means. "Over here, it brought everything right back down to earth, which is needed occasionally," said Rhodes to *Music and Sound Output*. "And then things started to break up. Punk became unfashionable, in fact almost overnight. It started in 1976, and by the end of 1978 it was dying. And that wasn't a bad thing," he concluded. As always happens in England, the demand rose up for new ideas and different ways of presenting them.

It was the dawning of a movement that would eventually be labeled New Romantic. Under this banner,

Duran Duran were initially introduced to the world. Yet they weren't looking for a category as much as a gathering place where they could find friendly company with other like-minded creative people. That place turned out to be the Rum Runner club. In addition to Duran Duran, the Rum Runner was home away from home for Birmingham's new young style setters, people who had had enough of punk's negativity and wanted to find new ways of feeling good about themselves. One way to pick up the mood of an evening was to dance, especially to the funky rhythms of black American bands like Chic, new wavers such as Talking Heads, and the techno-rock synthesizer-based beat of the important German quartet, Kraftwerk. Those who danced to this brave new music wanted clothes to match their hopeful mood.

These feelings started springing up all over England by the late 1970s. Every few weeks, word would travel among friends of a new club—usually an out-of-the-way place taken over by a free-wheeling entrepreneur one night a week. The sessions, which started at nine or so and lasted until the wee hours of the morning, were built around musical themes: jazz-funk on Tuesday, Bowie night on Thursday, etc. In order to keep out what they sneered at as "tourists"—people who wanted in mainly to stare at the regulars—the clubs followed the example laid down by New York's infamous Studio 54, and recruited doormen. If you looked exciting, you got in. If not, no amount of money could buy passage into those dark enclaves.

In London, the main clubs were places like Blitz, where Steve Strange, who recorded with his own group Visage, kept an eye on the door. At around the same time Duran Duran were completing their lineup in Birmingham, Spandau Ballet formed in London, and became the first recording artists associated with New Romanticism. Often, the two bands were linked together, because they were young, attractive, dressed by designers of the movement, and played rhythmic music. Spandau, however, were more strictly a dance band at the time, and as Nick pointed out, "If there hadn't been a Spandau Ballet then, there couldn't have been New Romantics, but there would have been a Duran Duran. . . . The fact that Spandau Ballet put their single out first and that they came from London had a lot of bearing on our first twelve months."

Elsewhere in Britain, the Human League were getting their first measure of success, and in Birmingham, the trendiest music fans started establishing their own hangouts. When Barbarella's lost its position as the city's top club, several different locations each attracted their own audience. The punks tended to stay at the Cedar Club, reggae fans went to another place, Handsworth, but the dress-up crowd needed its refuge. First, they stopped by the Hawkins Wine Bar and the Hosteria to eyeball the newest clothes, but by night-time, settled into Paul and Michael Berrow's Rum Runner club, which the brothers were running like the New York discos they loved. "It came to pass," recalled Paul Berrow early in Duran Duran's career, "that one of these evenings was a modern Bowie/Bryan Ferry night." Wearing outfits bought at designers Kahn & Bell, the stylish set, often cattily referred to as poseurs, discovered the Rum Runner—and in so doing, gave Duran Duran their earliest local support.

After Simon Le Bon took the final plunge and dropped out of college, the Berrow brothers began their management work in earnest. From the start, Duran Duran agreed that no one would be treated as a leader; all songs, credits, and royalties would be shared among the five—a fact they strongly feel has kept them close friends, despite the inevitable tensions of international fame. The group's first show under the current lineup was at the 1980 Edinburgh Summer Festival, followed by many local appearances. Naturally, they were familiar faces at the Rum Runner; but Duran Duran also performed in rival nightspots, such as the punk-oriented Cedar Club and the Holy City Zoo, a disco set underneath an old railway station.

Eventually, Duran Duran started acquiring dates in London, among them a night at the prestigious Marquee Club and as opening act for punk poet John Cooper Clarke in the two-thousand-capacity Lyceum ballroom. With the "New Romantic" network spreading via the press as quickly as punk had been publicized four years earlier, the band's connection with the Rum Runner followed them around. Although they didn't mind being constantly introduced as "Duran Duran from the Rum Runner," Nick Rhodes made it clear that he and his fellow players didn't ever want to restrict their audiences to the "poseurs."

"Just so long as people don't take it as our sole aim in life to be connected with the club," he told a reporter from *The Face*. "Our music is not an expression of the Birmingham scene, it's an expression of us." Although Duran Duran's democratic attitude towards their audiences would assist their popularity in America, it may have worked against them in style-defined Britain. Fortunately, the band's attractiveness and determination worked in their favor—as did a huge slice of managerial sacrifice.

Despite the unparalleled success of many bands who hail from every part of the U.K., starting with Liverpool's Beatles over fifteen years earlier, it was never easy for an artist away from London to get record company attention. Then as now, an eager band had few choices: They could stay where they lived, hoping that an open-minded record company talent spotter or press person would hear about them and come to see a gig; they could deluge London record labels with demo tapes, hoping that at least one would become excited; they could form their own label and concentrate on building a local reputation; or they could take on perhaps the most difficult and expensive option and tour.

Aware that remaining trend-setters in Birmingham might limit the kind of broad based appeal they really wanted to earn, Duran Duran decided to stress live shows. Two record labels were somewhat interested in the band but, as Spandau Ballet seemed to be drawing all the stylistic attention, neither of them was ready to give Duran Duran a commitment. And the group really didn't wish to spend any more time—not to mention their nonexistent budget—recording another demo tape, which the Berrows would then have to peddle around London, hat in hand. Knowing that clubs, too, had serious limitations ("We didn't want to play without many lights and bad sound," said Nick), Duran Duran strived for the big sell—opening act on a major British tour.

Their rescuer from obscurity was a rather unlikely choice. Singer Hazel O'Connor was certainly popular, but she was also controversial. A petite blonde girl who rose to prominence with the punks, Hazel was as much of an actress as a singer. Pretty girls have always had trouble being taken seriously in the British music business (which is even more chauvinistic than the American), and Hazel's fate was no exception. The press used to laugh at her for not being serious and gloomy enough, yet she identified with the spiky-haired black leather contingent, and her leading film role, as the star of *Breaking Glass*, totally immersed itself in the world of punk. More insular punkettes, like Siouxsie of the Banshees, had turned down the part, but Hazel's decision to tackle it proved to be a wise one. Unkind comments or not, *Breaking Glass* was a smash hit in English cinemas, and its soundtrack album also sold well. When Hazel commenced her British tour in November, 1980, she was at the height of her popularity.

O'Connor was quite agreeable to taking the young Birmingham quintet on tour as her opening act, but they would have to pay their own way. Everyone in the group understood that performing across Britain

could give Duran Duran the diverse exposure they
needed so badly, and no one balked about going without. It was at this point that Michael Berrow performed
an act which distinguishes the exploitative manager
from the one who really believes in his artists—he
mortgaged his home in Birmingham for twenty thousand pounds in order to finance Duran Duran's ex-
penses for the tour.

Whatever money Berrow raised by this noble ges-
ture was stretched into funding the band on the road
for over a month, right up until Christmas. They were
elated to be performing away from their regular Birmingham haunts and the occasional London venue,
even though Hazel attracted a hardcore punk crowd
on the strength of her movie, and Simon, in particular
as frontman, had to constantly dodge flying gobs of
spit. (That was the way punk audiences showed their
appreciation, or anger, or just plain indifference to
whoever was on stage. Unpleasant as it could be, the
bands all got used to it and disciplined themselves not
to take the flying pellets personally.)

Aside from the rough crowds they faced every night,
Duran Duran lived meagerly throughout the weeks they
traveled with Hazel. No one had very much nourishing
food to eat, and sleeping quarters were downright dia-
bolical. The band was salaried at the almost unlivable
rate of twenty dollars each per week, and home was
their camper bus, all five sleeping squashed together.
So after a long day of travel, the group had to set up
their own equipment, do a hasty sound check if there
was time, try to please a difficult audience, then unload
the gear and pack it into the van, find some sort of late
night cafe that was cheap enough for their budget, and
sleep, as the van bumped along the motorway to the
next destination. Oh yes, and they somehow had to
manage to find places to bathe and clean their clothes
since, after all, Duran Duran were known to be stylish
and had a reputation to uphold!

Small inconveniences aside, Duran Duran's supporting tour of Hazel O'Connor was to prove very astute, which the band realized as the rewards of their labor began to mount up. First of all, Hazel, who had taken more than a few hard knocks herself, was kind and fair to the group, all of whom were just a little younger than she. Refusing to join the cackles of fellow trendies in picking fun at O'Connor, the band shared Nick's sentiments that, "For what she does, she's really good. She's a great entertainer. Hazel was very good to us on that tour," he added, "and that is where we really learned how to play live." Duran Duran needed to know that they could challenge an audience who had never heard of them and disdained the scene they were part of—and by the end of their set, have won them over to some degree. Recalled Andy, "We had to go out and play a major tour with somebody we couldn't get bracketed with because of the distance between us musically, but with enough fans to put us up on a big stage in front of two thousand people for three weeks solid."

From these experiences, the band knew that not only did they like to tour, they were good at it—an attitude which has only been strengthened as Duran Duran's popularity extended to every corner of the world. Far from many of their rivals in the hipness sweepstakes, who foolishly proclaimed that live dates were out of fashion (notably, Spandau Ballet have really changed their tune on that subject since then), Duran Duran intended to do live performances every year. And they didn't demand, like some others, that those who wished to see them had to dress up; a follower who came to the show in casual shirt and jeans was equally welcome. "We believe in our music one hundred percent," John declared, "but we believe in complete individuality, too. It's all a question of style and developing what suits you best."

As a result of the tour, others outside Duran Duran's

circle started to believe in the band's potential. Naturally, their nervous families, who despaired of rock and rolling sons ever being able to forge a career from music, were overjoyed. John, who'd nearly been tossed out of his house only a few months earlier, was now the subject of pride. But on a much larger scale, three London based record labels who'd been notoriously resistant to Duran Duran's appeal vied to sign them once the tour was over. The leader of the pack was EMI's Dave Ambrose, who saw the group several times with Hazel O'Connor and offered them a worldwide contract. They were each given a wage of one hundred dollars—very generous for young musicians in their circumstances.

Consequently, the group were now in a position to stay off the road and tighten up the material which would comprise their first single, "Planet Earth," and LP. EMI even gave Duran Duran their own label, TRI-TEC, furthering their distinctive image as a group not meant for existing categories. "We ended up a lot better off because we got exactly what we wanted," Nick enthused about their new contract. "We signed for exactly the amount of money we wanted and managed to get control over items like album covers, who produces us, how many records we release a year, and so on. We were patient and it paid off."

Duran Duran vowed to live up to this newest and biggest responsibility, as they'd done on a less grand scale previously. For ten hours a day, they rehearsed the first songs that were to be recorded, "Planet Earth" and its follow-up, "Careless Memories," as well as several other tracks which would be included in their first album, straightforwardly titled *Duran Duran*. As 1980 drew to a close, the band closeted themselves in the Red Bus studio with producer Colin Thurston, and set about creating the next step towards Duranization of planet Earth. From the start, they wanted to grab the largest possible audience, and knew that there was a lack of good entertainers around—bands which showed a positive outlook for people who were seeking things to feel good about. The group perceived a gap for teen heroes in England, America, and Japan.

They knew what they wanted. Now, Duran Duran had the awesome task ahead of them of going after it.

ONE SMALL
PART OF
PLANET EARTH

*A*s the cold winter of 1981 pressed on, Duran Duran huddled in their studio, putting the finishing touches on "Planet Earth" and polishing up the songs intended for the debut album. Except for one unexpected show at London's Lyceum, in which they opened for classic pop band Sweet, Duran Duran kept a low profile. However, all about them controversy raged, having to do with clothes, image, hangouts, ideals, and all the other trappings of style which were then headline news in England. Encouraged by Britain's headline-hungry pop news weeklies, the growing movement was labeled Blitz Kids, Cult with No Name, and of course, New Romantics.

Duran Duran didn't mind being called "New Romantics" for a while; truth is, they *were* new, and they all considered themselves to be romantic, if that meant standing for the nicer aspects of life. The group weren't about to deny their good looks, and enjoyed dressing in a way which highlighted them. Not since the David Bowie "glitter rock" era did guys so openly wear makeup, and it became hard to imagine Nick or Simon without their sooty eye shadow accents. In a related move which they later felt might have been a mistake, Duran Duran hired alternative fashion editor Perry Haines, who headed up a streetwise magazine called *I-D*, as their "style consultant." Since Perry also worked for Spandau Ballet and Steve Strange, the chief London trendsetters, Duran Duran found themselves hard-pressed to establish their individuality in appearance, though once people heard the music, the Birmingham group's uniqueness was obvious. John Taylor was painfully aware of the image problem from which the group suffered, when he half joked, "Nobody's ever quite sure what to make of us. They never really knew whether we were five Polaroids that EMI Records had got together, or whether we were the new Queen."

Arriving in Birmingham to meet with journalists who now traveled in droves to this unlikely style center, the members of Duran Duran tended to dress in the following manner early in 1981: Simon, as a Mexican bandito—hair darkened, heavy eye makeup, silver gunbelt glistening, headband restraining his bouncing locks. Roger Taylor and Nick Rhodes tended to be more magazine-model glamorous, wearing light colored baggy suits. Nick's hair ran the gamut from blond to wilder shades of orange, and he wore equally brassy eye makeup. Almost always, Rhodes' figure was topped with a broad-brimmed hat, giving him a "gangster from the twenty-fifth century" look that demanded attention. John Taylor, fearful of appearing so faultless that he'd make the neighborhood girls feel like competitors, sometimes deliberately tousled his hair into wildness. John's taste was away from coordinated suits, more to the bright shirts, scarves, and leather jackets that the "glam" groups had popularized.

And Andy—well, Andy Taylor was the odd man out, though no one really minded. He'd pose in all the stylish gear and fit in with his colleagues onstage, but left to himself, might turn up in an old denim jacket with the faint traces of a heavy rock band logo still visible. Duran Duran, amongst themselves, never intended to be slaves, either to fashion or to music.

When "Planet Earth" was released in England on February 2, 1981, the band's insistence on blazing their own musical road to renown was apparent. The song lived up to Duran Duran's vow that it be danceable, but without imitating the overused thud-thud-thud of rival funky outfits. There was that bop-bop-bop chorus just ripe for singing along with or handclapping, yet Simon's vocals were no mere machine, as he performed the lyrics with bravado and emotion. "It's all about waking up," Le Bon curiously described the song.

One might enjoy Duran Duran on the dance floor, but they were just as interesting when sitting at home in front of the stereo. "We want to make dance music," Nick Rhodes explained, over and over. "We like disco, but the melodies seem to be weak. That's where our interests are." In fact, believing that the original version of "Planet Earth" was fine for home use or playing on radio, but didn't have enough drive for a club, the band released a heart-clutching elongated version of the song with a disco orientation. "It's more influenced by New York disco than British disco," Rhodes enthused, before he had ever set foot in America. "It's faster and more high energy. I mean, when they play 'Planet Earth' in the clubs, the dance floor is instantly crowded," the ex-disc jockey noted.

Slowly, "Planet Earth" started moving up the British charts, and Duran Duran wasted no time setting out on their first head-lining tour, eighteen English dates in February and March. Thrilled to be appreciated for themselves at last, the group set about dazzlingly pleasing their audiences, trying to ignore the sourheads who resented a band that enjoyed a personal rapport with their fans. If there is one attitude which has distinguished Duran Duran from their fellow romantics, it's the Birmingham group's enjoyment of the people who come to see them. Simon Le Bon is not interested in sneering at his audiences; he talks to them, smiles broadly and often, and within the bounds of safety, reaches out to touch their grabbing hands. "Some bands might like to stand at doors and restrict entry, but we happen to think that's wrong," Simon said flatly.

This may not have sat well with more remote artists,

who tended to isolate themselves with fancy lights and visual displays, but Duran Duran's message was received and appreciated by at least one reviewer. *Melody Maker* reporter Steve Sutherland saw the band's first headlining appearance at London's Sundown, a middle-sized hall, and didn't try to hide his enthusiasm: "A short, sweet set of memorable, unpretentious pop songs that pack real punch live and will sound so great on the radio that they'll put the rest of their chosen contemporaries to shame." Although the group were probably not thrilled with Sutherland's dislike of Simon's vocal style or the way Le Bon danced, they chose to highlight the positive qualities mentioned— their brightness and enjoyment of what they were doing.

While arguments continued to flourish regarding the band's looks and what movement they belonged to, Duran Duran preferred to keep a low profile, back at home in Birmingham. "Planet Earth" was followed two months later by "Careless Memories," and videos were shot for both. Russell Mulcahy began his lengthy directorial association with the group on "Planet Earth," though its familiar London setting didn't even hint at the exotic locations Mulcahy would explore with the band in future projects. The *I-D* crew of Perry Haines and Terry Jones directed "Careless Memories," which marked the high point of their association with the group. "Careless Memories" didn't match the modest success of "Planet Earth," disappointing Simon in particular, as the song is one of his favorites amongst the early recordings.

Nevertheless, hopeful that their first album would prove, once and for all, that the group wasn't simply an anonymous collection of attractive young men, *Duran Duran* was released in June. Shortly before the band embarked on another round of British dates, coupled with a handful of European festivals, they shot a third video, "Girls on Film," with 10 cc founders Lol Creme and Kevin Godley. From that point on, Duran Duran didn't have to look towards any outside events for their name to generate strong opinion. The album set the musical standard by which Duran Duran would be known, and "Girls on Film" put the staid world on notice that videos were going to be a major factor in making this band famous...and infamous.

The album indicated, for a start, that Duran Duran were not meant to be jumbled in with their more cultish rivals. Spandau Ballet's early albums and the recordings of Visage, Steve Strange's group, were beat-centered to the exclusion of almost everything else. The others certainly did not have anything akin to what Steve Sutherland called "Andy Taylor's power chord, axe-hero histrionics (that) steal the show," preferring to confine themselves to a more detached, synthesizer orientation. At the height of the new romantic era when it was practically a sin to be labeled a "rock" band (as opposed to being "modern"), John Taylor unashamedly declared, "If rock means power and drive excitement and showbiz, then yeah, we are a rock band, and we're only too happy to be called that." No matter how unfashionable the press wanted to make it seem, Duran Duran identified themselves as being a commercial group—and it hasn't exactly hurt them, long after many of their detractors have either faded away or gone just as commercial, like Spandau Ballet.

The songs on *Duran Duran*, composed so that everyone in the band shared in their creation, were very personal outpourings—especially to Simon, who writes most of the lyrics. At first, he explained, John also wrote some lyrics, but Le Bon—his theatrical background coming through—felt that he'd do a more convincing job singing his own words. "What is important is that I believe in the words I'm singing," he said. "Some of my songs, like 'Careless Memories' and 'Friends of Mine,' are very personal. They come from feelings which have been inside me for a long time, and now I've got a vehicle to get them outside. How other people interpret them will depend on their experiences." The band was eager to create a variety of feelings on their album, not just simple dance tunes, however much they love them. So *Duran Duran* also featured the Middle-Eastern flavored "Tel Aviv," which incorporated a string arrangement played by members of the London Philharmonic and Symphony Orchestras.

Working towards their very important goal of writing about personal feelings and emotions, Duran Duran made up their minds early on to stay away from politics. This wasn't a superficial decision, and it caused the band a lot of aggravation—both in England at the hands of other bands, and later in America, where they were challenged by the press. Having just gone through the wrenching experiences of the punk era, when not even the Queen was spared the punks' venom, many English young people had politically awakened. By the hundreds of thousands, British teenagers graduated from school at age fifteen and were unable to get a job. They dismally viewed the prospects of a lifetime on the "dole" (unemployment compensation). For a group like Duran Duran to sing about lost loves and fantasize about mystical hideaways, was angrily branded as escapism.

Understandably sensitive to the accusations, Duran Duran staunchly defended their choice to be apolitical, but were mature enough, even at their ages, not to lash out against those who did put social comment in the forefront. When pressured to do so, Simon or Nick will admit that, of course as individuals, they have opinions about current events, but do not wish to use their position as popular musicians to mix the two. "Our own political views have nothing to do with our music," said Nick when asked the meaning of "Planet Earth."

"If the bomb drops, it drops. We're getting out there and making the best of what's here. If someone doesn't do that then everyone will go insane sitting at home thinking about it. . . . We want people to have fun. Enjoy themselves, relax, and be entertained by us."

Simon was even more emphatic, insisting to a *Smash Hits* reporter, "Nobody's actually going to get anywhere by worrying. The post-punk rock people with a special message, the guys who got up onstage and preached—you've got a very small converted audience who will enjoy that in a masochistic kind of way." Fortunately, as times changed, the charts found room for both preachers and entertainers, so the pop wars have subsided a bit.

However, Duran Duran had some other problems to clear out of the way before they could relax and feel like the stars they were becoming. One huge stumbling block was to be their "Girls on Film" video, which is eye-riveting mainly because of all the semi-naked young ladies tussling with one another that it reveals. Before they set off for America, Simon was hopeful that the United States would be ready for Duran Duran's happy dance spirit. He kept careful note of American club playlists and saw that the band's three videos were doing particularly well, especially in New York. Even though their first U.S. clubs might be small, the group anticipated wonderful things happening there.

Duran Duran arrived in America for the first time in September, 1981, and two days later—still dazed and completely unprepared for the size, scale, and pace of the country—were introduced to a packed room of reporters at Capitol Records' New York office. Before the band arrived, journalists had been shown the videos of "Planet Earth," "Careless Memories," and "Girls on Film." There weren't too many women in the room, but those present were very offended by "Girls on Film," and it was one of the main items the group was challenged about. Besides the press, MTV, which had only been launched weeks earlier, felt "Girls on Film" was too revealing. Though the channel would become one of Duran Duran's biggest advocates, it decided to ban "Girls on Film" until the song was reedited without the near nudity.

The other problem, however, really wasn't the

band's fault. Weary of being called "New Romantics" for the better part of a year in Britain, Duran Duran had finally planned to disassociate themselves from the cult. They were playing to audiences of all types, not just those who could pass muster in front of a snooty doorman. Their fans tended to be younger and more diversified than those the "Blitz Kids" pulled in, and at the bottom line, Duran Duran didn't see anything wrong with being openly commercial about what they did for a living. Imagine, then, the shock on their five faces when they walked into Capitol's conference room and found themselves sitting under posters that blared, "Duran Duran! England's New Romantic Rebels." The "escapist" questions started up in earnest, and in a country where they'd hoped to avoid it completely, Duran Duran were again faced with being new romantic spokesmen.

"Back then the whole image was forced upon us," Nick Rhodes told me when I interviewed the band for *Creem* a year later and brought up their difficult U.S. debut. "We got here and even the record company had those posters up. We couldn't believe it," he said, rolling his eyes in helplessness. "Especially," added Simon, "after all the hard work we put into England to get people to call us by our own name, for us to come over here and the exact thing happens—we went 'Oh-my-God-this-is-really-bad.'"

But Duran Duran were thrilled to be in America, under whatever image they were billed. New York was a dream come true for the five go-getters, who explored every corner of Manhattan and quickly discovered how much they enjoyed the American way of life. John, who gravitates to good food wherever he goes, fell in love with heaping bacon and egg breakfasts—and had to work extra hard on gigs to keep his muscular physique from getting too chunky! Taylor also was enthralled by U.S. television, and the novelty of twenty-four-hour-a-day late movies kept him up many a night. Rather overwhelmed by New York prices, the group (who earned one hundred dollars a week) tried to deal with sleeping in rooms costing one hundred dollars per *night* at the St. Moritz Hotel, overlooking Central Park.

Of course, the band's biggest late night excitement were the shows they played, which commenced September 18 and 19 at New York's number-one dance club, the Ritz. Possibly if Duran Duran had realized how strong their appeal would become to teenagers, they'd have picked another club; the Ritz has an over-18 door policy. On the other hand, playing at the Ritz immediately stamped Duran Duran as hot up-and-comers, and there would be plenty of other shows in the months to come at which all ages were welcome.

Although the group's sound monitors gave them some trouble in hearing themselves during the sets, the Ritz audiences were very satisfied. The club reminded John of the Venue, a well thought of London nightspot, and he was especially pleased by the huge numbers of people who turned up on those foggy September nights. "The guard said they were over the fire risk," said Nick, grinning. "People came backstage and shouted, 'Hey man, it was really great!' I really like New Yorkers because they're so enthusiastic. I love the way they dance at a gig, they really go crazy...." Naturally, "Planet Earth," their best known song in America at that point, was the show's odds-on favorite, generating the loudest cheers.

Duran Duran made the most of their first, too short trip to the United States, playing in Los Angeles after New York, then returning to the Big Apple, where they visited in-spot Studio 54—the same disco that had sparked their managers on the idea of theme nights and bop-till-you-drop, but fashionably. Nick fulfilled his dream of meeting artist/hanger-outer-par-excellence Andy Warhol, who was very taken with the band. Nick decided that Warhol's autobiography, *From A to B and Back Again*, was his favorite book, and frequently carried it with him. Faced with unimaginable luxuries that they couldn't even have imagined 10 months earlier as they lay squashed together in their touring bus, the group ordered fantastic meals of lobster, paté, steak, shrimp—and couldn't even finish them. So this was the U.S.A.! More understandable was their happy discovery that Space Invaders and Asteroids were cheaper to play here than back home.

So successful on the whole was the group's premier American visit that, when they returned to Britain to gear up for the next string of home dates, only one disturbing memory nagged at the band. To the loyal circle of Duran Duran fans in the United States who bought the album and singles and attended their concerts, the group were heroes. But America wasn't England, and there's an awful lot of space between New York and California. Out there, and even outside of the limited hip circles on the two coasts, Duran Duran were invisible. What was a "Cult With No Name" in Britain was hardly even worth finding a name for in America. Adam Ant's pirate clothing had caught on a little bit, but Duran Duran were frustrated by a musical brick wall that seemed to exist, and swore that they'd eventually break through it.

"I want to be Number One in the album charts simultaneously in America and Britain," Nick said grandly, as the group returned to their hideaways in Birmingham. "1995, here we come," he joked, little imagining that his prediction would take only two more years to come true. "I really want to shake up America," Simon replied with grim determination. "Musically, they're in the Dark Ages. They think they're the center of the world out there and that everybody else revolves around them. When you get there you feel like slapping them in the face and shouting, 'Look around you! There are other things that matter, too.'" Luckily for him, Simon saved this mini-fit of temper for home, and showed a sunny face to the Americans. Anyway, by the time the band returned the following summer, they would be making headway at a much faster pace. Duran Duran capped their first full year of success by releasing a fourth single and video from the debut album, "My Own Way," and headlining fourteen dates in Britain throughout December.

The English tour included two shows in one of London's top rock halls, the Hammersmith Odeon, and three more in their very own Birmingham Odeon, but none could have meant more than the triumphant post-show party Duran Duran threw at the Rum Runner. Signposts on tiny white balloons tied to lampposts in the street read, "Duran Duran Live at the Rum Runner Tonight." By evening's end, champagne flowed in the aisles. Strangely, a visiting London journalist found that the scene was much less snobby than an equivalent celebration in his home town would have been, despite the visible presence of the band's entourage, friends, hangers-on, and girls, girls, girls—all looking their fashionable best.

Trying hard not to think about the hangovers they'd all be dealing with come morning, the band considered how unbelievably well 1981 had treated them, and how they'd helped to make their own luck. Since January, the group had largely severed their connection to any musical or social labels, done two British and one American tour, had four decent-selling singles including the hit "Planet Earth," and released a debut album no one would ever have to be ashamed of. Yes, reflected Rhodes, carefully choosing his words despite the quantity of partying he'd been doing, this year had not been bad at all. "We've always put a lot of thought into Duran Duran, to try and prepare the ground properly. We could have made an independent single early on, which would probably have done our credibility with the rock press a lot of good. But we always knew that the sound we wanted required a big studio and a good producer, so we decided to wait until the time was right. If you approach the business like that," Nick told a *Record Mirror* reporter, "then you're much better prepared to grab the opportunities when they arise and not look back afterwards and say, 'If only we'd done...' like too many groups do."

Simon also knew that when the results were added up, all the gloss attached to a "scene" didn't mean anything unless the music was there first. And, he said proudly at the Rum Runner, the sound was more important to establish before anything else. So if Duran Duran piled on the makeup and the fancy hairdos and elaborate designer clothing, one could start doubting their sincerity—until the power of their performances removed any hesitations. Nothing except Duran Duran's own limitations would hold them back, and as far as the band was concerned, they were never going to stop. "It would be nice to get ten years out of this," Andy said. Roger expressed what everyone knew deep down: "We're totally confident. We're going to crack it big."

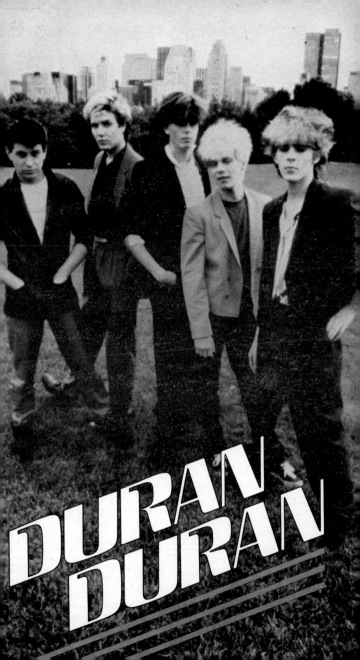

Previous page: New York City became Duran Duran's home away from home when they toured during 1982. With the Big Apple's towers behind them, the guys enjoy a sunny day in Central Park.

Left: Showing off Anthony Price's designer military gear as they celebrated Christmas at the Rum Runner.

*L*eft: Where it all began. Duran Duran relax at the Rum Runner around the time their first album was released.

EBET ROBERTS

*T*he tour that launched a million screams (above)! Duran Duran onstage in Chicago, singing a tune from *Seven and the Ragged Tiger.*

*V*intage Simon
Le Bon at the
Ritz, 1981.

Pier 84 (below), in summer 1982. This fairly calm shot must have been taken before the wave of telephone numbers started landing on the stage!

JUSTIN THOMAS

EBET ROBERTS

As he and Andy work on the Rio sessions (above), Nick Rhodes proudly wears a T-shirt advertising Andy Warhol's film Bad...or is he trying to tell us something?

Below: Of course we wear our own T-shirts, too, John seems to be saying. Nothing our fans buy wouldn't suit us!

PAUL NATKIN/PHOTO RESERVE

JOHN BELLISSIMO

*H*aving just arrived in America,
Duran Duran appeared a bit
overwhelmed by the size and pace
of the country.

Right: Duran Duran's mystery man, Roger Taylor. Below: At a return to the old haunt, the band play a special Christmas show for fans.

JUSTIN THOMAS

LAURIE PALADINO

Simon Le Bon and Andy Taylor are caught in the act. Obviously, they believe in the power of good, honest sweat!

EBET ROBERTS

*J*ust keep staring at my iridescent suit, Nick commands (below), and I'll have you in my power! Right: A job well done....

JOHN BELLISSIMO

VINNIE ZUFFANTE/STAR FILE

*R*ight: Andy and John happily sign copies of their video 45 at the infamous 1983 Times Square event. Little do they know that the only way out of the packed city block will be to dig a tunnel underneath....

JUSTIN THOMAS

Right: Andy and Tracey dressed all in white for a charity ball held at Christmastime in London's posh Embassy Club, a favorite band hangout.

DURAN
DURAN
ANDY TAYLOR 4

A man and his guitars (above). Andy Taylor poses amid the fulfillment of his impossible dream. Right: When "Hungry Like the Wolf" shot up the British charts, Duran Duran made one of their many visits to Top of the Pops. It's okay Simon, you don't have to beg—we'll buy your records!

JUSTIN THOMAS

ANDRE CSILLAG/RETNA LTD.

*G*rateful to have escaped rampaging Sri Lankan elephants and Antiguan tarantulas, Duran Duran set forth (right) to eat their way through the Land Down Under.

JUSTIN THOMAS

THE BIG
BREAKTHROUGH

*I*f 1981 offered Duran Duran a hint of what lay beyond their Birmingham homes, the new year would eventually give them the whole world in technicolor, its sights, sounds, and smells lending an exotic allure to the down home British boys. First on the agenda would be a new album. Though most of its songs had yet to be written, the band already had a title in mind: *Rio*, thought of by John. Duran Duran's record company press release, which accompanied the album, referred to "Rio" as the band's "collective dream woman," and it's certainly true that images of lovely ladies are an ongoing part of the group's style and flavor. In fact, the cover painting of *Rio* was done by Los Angeles artist Patrick Nagel, whose work they had glimpsed in *Playboy*.

"We didn't want to stick another picture of the band on the cover," Nick pointed out to a *Trouser Press* reporter. "We wanted to use an artist. We gave Patrick the title *Rio* and said, 'Do a girl who goes with that.'" Nagel's special insight resulted in the ruby lipped, dark-haired beauty who makes the *Rio* sleeve stand out from its competition. The band was so impressed by the album's cover art that they even wanted to give away a print of it with each LP, but the idea proved too costly.

However, Duran Duran had been deeply affected

by their visits to America over the last year and that, too, found its place in *Rio*, particularly the title song. Simon remembers being warned by friends that the group would get mugged the moment they stepped off the plane, but instead they found the U.S. to be a welcoming, eye-opening experience. "So the song's all about the good things here; there's the line, 'From the mountains in the north down to the Rio Grande.'" Simon added: "*Rio* is a celebration of America. What we liked was how honest the people were and how different and colorful the country was. We wanted to make something that was optimistic. That was the mood we were aiming for."

When Duran Duran began work in London's AIR Studios, with producer Colin Thurston once again at the helm, they were confident that *Rio* would more than live up to expectations as a follow-up to *Duran Duran*. Even though, unlike the first album, the band was now feeling pressure from outside as well as within themselves to make a record of quality, they knew that their writing and playing skills had improved with experience.

According to Simon Le Bon, the problem of establishing themselves in the States actually helped when it came time to record *Rio*. "It's the reason the second album is so much better than the first," the singer proudly confided in an interview. "When John and Roger went into the studio to put down the original bass and drum tracks on *Rio*, they were so tight from touring that everything was absolutely spot-on instead of nearly spot-on. We had gained confidence by the end of that first U.S. tour. It's like a kid being thrown in at the deep end of a swimming pool. You struggle for a while and then you learn. Also," he said, having the gift of hindsight, since when we spoke *Rio* was racing up the charts, "success obviously helps you relax a little more."

Except for "The Chauffeur," for which Simon had written the lyrics as a freestanding poem way back in

1978, before he even joined the group—all the songs on *Rio* were written to order. Nick recalled that everyone had to make a sincere effort to keep the new songs sounding natural. Where *Duran Duran* was created without any groundwork, *Rio* had a reputation to uphold. "We don't want to consciously rewrite the first album," commented Rhodes. "I think there's a tendency to get very indulgent because of the first album's success. Then you might tend to start meandering and do anything for the sales." Roger added that as musicians, the group were becoming more aware of each other, and *Rio* would reflect that.

From the start, Duran Duran were concerned that each member of the group would be appreciated for his special contributions. "We had seen too many groups where one or two people dominated the songwriting, got most of the royalties, and angered the other members of the group," Nick said. Therefore, even though Simon writes all the lyrics, the writing royalties are shared equitably. Before Le Bon scribbles anything into his "big thick book full of lyrics," everyone works on the melodies.

One reason why Duran Duran songs have such pulling power is the importance given the chorus. Everyone knows very well that if fans can't sing along with the chorus straightaway, they might as well toss out the tune. From that starting point, a song slowly evolves. No one is afraid to critique someone's suggestion, and according to Nick, any idea has to be accepted by everyone in order to be good for the song. "It's totally ruthless," said Rhodes with a laugh, heartily enjoying the healthy competitive spirit.

Once the music is done, Maestro Le Bon starts to imagine words that will heighten its mood, and the group pretty much accepts his lyrics as a finished product. Said Simon about the way in which he writes, "The songs I like best are the ones where you feel that someone is watching a scene from a movie, or looking through the window and capturing something that's actually happening. . . . I like to imply things in a subtle way. It's like painting an abstract picture; I like to suggest, not outline." Anyone who has wondered why Duran Duran's videos often seem to offer a mystical, dreamlike state need look no further than Simon's perspective on writing, which gives the group's songs vast shadings of color.

Satisfied with the quality of *Rio*, which John felt was "probably the first real Duran Duran album because it's honestly us," the group left Britain in search of faraway locales to film videos for the album. Simon knew exactly where he wanted to go, and a holiday without work was much too expensive for him to consider at this stage, so Le Bon wrote a few songs about Sri Lanka. Then with video director Russell Mulcahy by their side, Simon, John, and Roger flew off to the small Indian Ocean island—the first stop in what amounted to nonstop traveling throughout 1982. Nick and Andy stayed in London to supervise the final mixing of *Rio*. By the time they flew out to Sri Lanka, the two had no chance to relax before they joined their colleagues to work on the videos.

In all, three of the band's most attention-getting videos were made in Sri Lanka: "Hungry Like the Wolf," "Save a Prayer," and "Lonely in Your Nightmare." From the instant they began shooting on the island, with its brilliant colors, lush foliage, and exotic animals providing a uniquely dramatic backdrop to the songs, the band knew that something special was being created. They also knew that, for all the discomforts and strangeness they'd experienced on the remote island (a lot), Sri Lanka was a place to be in right now, not five years later. "The jet set of the Western World leave their grubby fingermarks all over a place, and as soon as they get their hands on Sri Lanka they'll mess that up as well, so we're going to get there first," said Simon. Consequently, after one of the Berrows visited the island on a vacation and came back raving about it, he was plied with questions. Yes, he recounted, there were temples and jungles—exactly what Duran Duran had wanted in their videos.

The action started early—six A.M., Nick remembered, thinking angrily of those back home who decided that the boys were having a little layabout in the sun and then, by the way, making some movies. The work days lasted at least twelve hours, and were sometimes even eighteen hours long, just as if a feature film were being shot. Shooting these videos was extremely costly, amounting to about $75,000 just for the time in Sri Lanka, and Duran Duran had to pay it up front, later to be reimbursed by the record company. Add to that an island temperature that regularly shot over one hundred degrees in daytime, and it's almost miraculous that the group didn't suffer more mishaps. There were, they all agreed, enough of those.

"We had to deal with things like unexpected tropical storms and a power outage on the last day of shooting, when we still had one crucial scene to do," Nick remembered. "The food in Sri Lanka was absolutely disgusting!" Roger exclaimed. Simon agreed. "As soon as I arrived in the place, I saw all this meat hanging up and I couldn't eat it. Some of the fish is okay, but you can't drink the water." Roger recalled that everywhere they went, people stared at the five of them—natives and tourists alike—unable to show the courtesy Duran Duran were used to receiving. Poor Roger was chosen to ride an elephant during one scene of "Save a Prayer." Looking at the finished video, Taylor seems to have struck up a healthy relationship with the beast. But the true story is that while the animal heard a playback of the song, it caught the scent of a female elephant and charged off towards its future mate at breakneck speed—with Roger on his back! Fortunately, the resourceful drummer managed to hang on until they passed a body of water and he jumped in. "If I hadn't landed in water, I would have broken my leg for sure. I shiver at the memory," said the usually fearless Taylor.

Elephants were to give the group's guitarists a hard time, as well. Sanitary conditions on Sri Lanka were far from modern, and Andy was accidentally given a drink that was contaminated by elephant urine. Although he sensed something wasn't quite right with his digestion, Taylor gamely chalked it up to his being in a strange climate and carried on with the band's grueling schedule. But the infection he was carrying would cause him terrible trouble in the weeks to come. John, meanwhile, was in the wrong place at the wrong time, and an elephant peed on him in a lake! "Stronger than the hotel shower, it was," he weakly joked. As bravely as explorers, Duran Duran risked their health by working in regions infested with malaria, but luckily, they were spared any further ailments. Well, there was the time, during "Save a Prayer," where the group all stood reverently before a Buddhist temple: when the cameras clicked off, five pairs of bare feet beat a hasty retreat from its scorched concrete ground.

From the primitive exoticism of Sri Lanka, Duran Duran jetted to Australia, a land equally rich in physical beauty but with totally modern cities, all packed with the band's followers. "Planet Earth" had reached number one in Australia, and their tour was completely sold out. For the first time, Duran Duran came face to face with massive hysteria, and everyone admitted that the chaos took some getting used to. Whenever any of the band stepped outside the hotel to shop or sightsee, a frantic wave of fans pursued him, often wrecking a shop or causing major traffic stoppages. "It's a weird thing," said Nick in a *Melody Maker* interview, "when you go out shopping and have to get the police in to get you back out of the shop." Added John, who frankly felt a tremendous sense of unease about how to deal with overzealous fans, "Sometimes you think you owe them a good night out because they've paid £5 for a ticket, you owe them a good record for their money, but what do you owe a kid who stands outside your hotel for twelve hours in the rain?

"Nine times out of ten we'll sign autographs, but what if there's one hundred of them? Do you owe it to them? That one time when you don't sign, do you feel bad about it? It's a very fine line." He sighed, wrestling with a problem that has only increased with time. Fortunately, Duran Duran's gigs always turned out so successfully and they pleased their audiences enough that the band was able to compensate for their total lack of privacy. The group particularly appreciated how much time the young Australians spent on their beautiful beaches, instead of sitting indoors all day with the TV on. And everyone raved, after dealing with the woes of Sri Lankan cuisine, that Australian food was wonderful: "The best steak, the best lamb, the best fish, the best prawn, the best fruit. The apples are like something out of *Gulliver's Travels*," raved a happy and well-fed Simon.

When the band reached Melbourne, they played to an ecstatic audience of over five thousand, who never realized that Andy Taylor was in serious trouble. Despite the ill feeling he had had ever since Sri Lanka, Andy insisted on giving his all to every show throughout Australia—then partying just as hard afterwards. Just before the encore, Taylor's legs buckled under him and Duran Duran ended the Melbourne show as a quartet. Following interim medical treatment, Andy joined the tour as it winged to Japan, a country so on top of things when it comes to hot new faces that Duran Duran were in for more mayhem. The Japanese had already put the group's faces onto buttons and pencil cases back in 1981, before they'd made much of an impact anywhere, and this tour far surpassed the early adulation.

In what was beginning to remind observers of the madness that surrounded the Beatles at every turn, Duran Duran were chased all over Japan by thousands of screaming girls. News of their hotels leaked out, and an army of Durannies constantly stood guard, poised to follow the band in taxis if someone ventured outside.

The Japanese tour concluded without incident, and Duran Duran briefly returned home, where they oversaw the final details before the single "Hungry Like the Wolf" and the album *Rio* were released, in May and June respectively. Andy, meanwhile, barely made it back to Britain before the bacterial illness he'd contracted in Sri Lanka and his nonstop pace on the Far East tour almost did him in. During one of the first weekends they were back, the group appeared on a television talk show. Andy went horseback riding the next day, but by midafternoon, he was running a 104-degree fever. John, receiving a frantic phone call from his friend, summoned a doctor, who diagnosed Andy as having malaria! He was rushed to the hospital by ambulance and in the course of his five day stay, had his ailment correctly identified as pyrexia—caused by a combination of exhaustion, self-neglect, and that wretched tainted water he'd drunk in Sri Lanka.

With Andy flat on his back for a while, the band postponed a European tour until the autumn, after they returned from America, which was next on their busy schedule. But before they departed England on their westward adventures, the group was delighted to note that "Hungry Like the Wolf" was soaring up the British chart, where it took a firm stand in the Top 10 by June.

Sensitive to their early press image with frilly shirts and exaggerated trousers, the band now fitted themselves out with the expensive, well-tailored designs of Anthony Price. But just to show that they didn't take their wardrobe (or themselves) too seriously, Duran Duran cheerfully allowed thousands of dollars worth of clothes to be soaked as they filmed two more videos in the Caribbean island of Antigua. Unlike the sometimes frightening conditions of Sri Lanka, Antigua offered the band exoticism and tropical beauty under somewhat more controlled circumstances. Director Russell Mulcahy was now an indispensable member of the Duran Duran family, and he directed the "Rio" and "Night Boat" videos in Antigua.

While pleased with the wide open sunshine feeling of "Rio" and the eerie, dusk hour sensation achieved in "Night Boat," even these far more relaxing locations weren't without risk to the band. Simon may have been smiling aboard the yacht on "Rio," but he was really quite seasick. And just as Roger was about to embrace a beautiful James Bond-ish woman on the beach, also for "Rio," his foot got bitten by a crab and Taylor toppled into the sea. After that, no one had any objections when it was time for Duran Duran to catch a jet to the U.S.A., and begin more than two solid months of touring. These were the shows which would lay the foundation for establishing Duran Duran as one of the 1980s first great bands.

Everyone knew that America was not going to be an easy sell. Unlike Britain, where new trends were regularly covered by radio and TV once they showed some action on the charts, new music had been having a tough time making headway in the States. Even the Beatles had been huge successes in England for a full year before Americans caught the Fab Fourmania. In the early 1970s, artists who had strings of number one singles at home in Britain—such as Slade and T-Rex—got barely a flicker of attention when they crossed the Atlantic. And when punk began, first in New York by the Ramones and then in England by the Sex Pistols, Clash, and other bands, American record labels and radio stations sullenly resisted the new sounds for years. By the time a few stations got around to airing the Pistols' classic thunderbolts, for example, the group was on the verge of breaking up.

So when the New Romantic banner carriers Spandau Ballet and Visage visited America, radio programmers dismissed their music as simply another short-lived trend. They had no way of knowing that Duran Duran would be any different and, to be honest, the old-line big shots didn't care. After all, *Duran Duran* hadn't sold very well in America, and "Planet Earth" was not a hit here, as it had been in other nations. The group had a surprisingly mature attitude about overcoming their image problems, as Simon explained in the midst of their 1982 tour. "You have to keep banging your head against the brick wall and chip it away, bit by bit, to make sure you work enough so that people will hear of you. There's no magical instant exposure anymore in the way the Beatles had it, because there're so many more bands around. And also, people were prepared to play the Beatles' stuff. They're not so willing now.

"I don't blame the radio for being cautious," Simon continued, far from angry. "'New Romantic' is such a lightweight phrase that radio stations were frightened of it, because they thought, this is gonna go for a week and sink the week after. And they're interested in bands that are going to be making records in a couple of years, at least. People they can play and back up and talk about." Despite the awesome obstacles they faced on the climb, Duran Duran were determined to crack American resistance by the time their tour was finished. "We want to be absolutely ace banana, number one famous," Simon said brightly. "We see touring America as a challenge, really—it's a very big country and when you're going to be the biggest pop group in the world, you might as well start in a big country!" Quite a cocky prediction at the time, and one which would take more than six months to start being fulfilled.

Meanwhile, Duran Duran set about getting the most enjoyment they could from America. New York became their base of operations for several regional dates, serving two purposes: the group loved the city, and it was the central point for Capitol Records' East Coast promotional efforts. Any day free of performing was devoted to interviews at open-minded radio stations (often low-budget college facilities, which gave the band lots of early support), with magazines and, increasingly, with the up-and-coming cable music channel MTV, which would eventually stand out as Duran Duran's strongest media ally.

Anyone who attended Duran Duran's show at New York's Pier 84 on June 25, 1982, knew that big things were in store for this band. Outside America, the group were acknowledged headliners, capable of drawing audiences in the thousands. But here the tables were turned, and for the first time in almost two years, Duran Duran were the opening act at large venues. One week later, on July 2, they'd pack the eight-hundred-capacity Peppermint Lounge very nicely on their own. However, at the Pier, they opened for zany Australian rock band Split Enz, to a capacity crowd of eight thousand sweaty souls. While a hefty percentage of the crowd at that show were guys who stood on top of their seats and applauded the band's musicianship, the girls at the front were going crazy. With only the stage's elevation and a few scattered police barricades to separate them from the group, dozens of girls crowded into the few feet in front of the first row of seats.

Positioning themselves in front of their favorite band member, the avid fans started tossing love objects to the stage: flowers, banners, photographs, telephone numbers, even the odd bit of lacy lingerie! For their part, Duran Duran took the attention in stride, smiling happily at the constantly undulating audience. Simon had only to crouch, flex a well toned arm, or sweetly grin to be half-drowned by a wave of screams. Runners-up for the fans' devotion seemed to be split between John Taylor, whose coolness contrasted with Le Bon's open warmth, and Nick Rhodes who, tucked behind his synthesizer, was a black-clad man of mystery. Yet no one was neglected at this remarkable show, as the hard-to-please guys showered their applause on Andy Taylor's guitar leads and Roger's relentless drumming. When the set ended, forty-five minutes later, as road crews hurried to prepare the stage for Split Enz, much of the audience was left open-mouthed at having received so much from a "mere" opening act.

By constantly showing determined cheer to their audiences, Duran Duran won respect as they criss-crossed the United States and Canada. On headlining dates, they played in clubs that were sometimes limited to just three hundred people. In order to reach larger groups and introduce them to Duran Duran music, the band agreed to open nine dates of a Blondie tour—which turned out to be one of the smartest moves they ever made. As it turned out, Blondie were on the downward side of their career, touring in support of their latest album release, *The Hunter*, which was not exactly burning up the charts. For them, the dates often verged perilously close to disaster, as many of the shows were poorly attended. Because of that, however, Duran Duran's energetic performances stood out in marked contrast to Blondie's insecure set.

Typical of the promising response given Duran Duran was the show they played at Toronto's mammoth CNE Stadium in August. Traditionally a home to the very biggest acts, the CNE can hold up to 35,000 people, but it was barely one-fifth full for Blondie's show. Yet when Duran Duran stepped out on that vast expanse, no one dreamed that the group was terrified. Athletic Simon bounded all over the huge stage as if he was born to it, encouraging the audience to move up front and get closer to him by calling out, "Do you have any idea what it feels like up here when everyone gets up and dances?" In response, they all joined hands with friends and leapt about as the band played "Hungry Like the Wolf" and "Rio." Duran Duran were called back for an encore with thunderous applause. Even Debbie Harry acknowledged, as Blondie began its show, that "Duran Duran gave me a hard act to follow."

Asked about their experiences touring America as an opening act. Simon preferred to remember it as a learning experience which ultimately benefitted the group. "The dates with Blondie were a great experience in terms of playing huge places." In Toronto, he said, "You could reach out and touch the audience at the front, but if you looked out towards the horizon there were people a football field away."

Le Bon pointed out that American audiences "come to see a band mainly to enjoy it all, and they listen to the support group too. Playing to such large audiences taught me how to work the crowds. I wouldn't call it a dying art, but a lot of bands work on the premise that their very appearance is enough to entertain. But I think you've got to treat them right," he declared.

The group reached California midway in the tour, and combined another huge wave of press, radio, and television interviews with some very special personal business. The interviews were more of what they had experienced in New York—smiling and being charming to dozens of hosts and reporters who wanted Duran Duran to explain why they weren't new romantics. The old legends took forever to die in America, passed along from one end of the vast country to the other and, as John was well aware, "The only way we can prove it is by playing to these people. It's a massive gamble, but we really do believe in old-fashioned sweat and toil. That's what The Police did, and, bar the Human League, they're the only new supergroup to have appeared in the last five years." It's estimated that Duran Duran's 1982 American tour cost them over $200,000, and throughout the summer *Rio* didn't even get near the Top 100.

Noting that the band's first recognition had come from dance clubs, Capitol Records brought in producer David Kershenbaum to remix four Duran Duran songs in extended dance versions. The EP, titled *Carnival*

and containing the new mixes of "Hungry Like the
Wolf," "Girls on Film," "Hold Back the Rain," and
"My Own Way," was released to America-only in July.
Though radio stations were again reluctant to give the
songs an airing, Capitol hung onto the remixed tracks.
When in late November *Rio* was reserviced to radio
stations with the new versions substituted, the results
would be staggering.

Meanwhile, the Duran Duran entourage was much
more concerned, as August approached, with a wedding in the family. Andy Taylor was eager to marry
his longtime girlfriend, Tracey Wilson, who he had first
met when she cut the band's hair. Said Andy, "There
were lots of girls in my life, but Tracey became the
one I felt most comfortable with. On my twenty-first
birthday [Feb. 16, 1982], I planned to celebrate at the
Rum Runner. Tracey was ill and stayed at my flat. Her
best friend was the one who suggested that it would
be a great idea if we got married. When I crawled in
at four in the morning, I asked Tracey if she wanted
to get married. She told me not to be so silly. The next
morning she said yes," Andy happily recalled.

Between Andy's recurring bouts with illness and the
band's nonstop touring schedule, arranging a wedding
required masterful planning. Rather than pull out of
the Blondie tour and have the wedding take place in
England, Andy convinced his bride-to-be to join him
in Los Angeles. Tracey left the Wolverhampton-based
haircutting business—Wilson, Wilson, & Wilson—in
the family's hands, and flew to California. Her one
regret was that, because of their business obligations,
Tracey's parents wouldn't be able to share the special
day, July 31, 1982, with their daughter.

The Berrow brothers, plus Roger and John, chipped
in to give the happy couple a wedding in grand style
(so grand, in fact, that it was front-page news back in
England). They rented out that Los Angeles landmark,
the Chateau Marmont, and all the band dressed for-

mally in top hats, morning coats, pearl tie pins, and pinstripe trousers. John, who stood up for Andy as best man, "shook like a leaf," the guitarist laughed. Among the presents given to the happy couple by their friends were a cigarette-pack-shaped light from Nick and a porcelain sake set, acquired during the Japanese tour by Simon. When the couple was wed, Tracey became a Taylor and Andy took Wilson as his middle name, a moving symbol of their deep devotion to one another.

Tracey's influence on Andy has been all for the best, as she has inspired him to cut down on the wild living. He's even become a vegetarian, as Tracey and her father run a charity home for animals at home in Birmingham. The most rootless member of Duran Duran had at last found the comforts of home and a family of his own.

The group returned home in September, pleased with the new musical skills that intensive touring had given them. They might have wished that America hadn't shown the second album such limited exposure—duplicating the fate of the first LP—but now it was time to concentrate on Europe, where stardom was already assured. Over six weeks, Duran Duran performed throughout Scandinavia, and in France, Belgium, Germany, and Holland. Only once did the enjoyment of touring turn sour, and that resulted from an offstage incident.

Roger Taylor is by far the shyest, least publicity seeking member of Duran Duran, so it was a dreadful irony that he came in for the only serious public attack ever made on anyone in the group. Of course, there were different versions of the assault story that came to light, but the most agreed-upon version has it that, after performing in Munich, several of the band were relaxing in a nearby club. Roger was accused of stealing someone's drink, a rather absurd charge considering that Duran Duran could have easily bought rounds for the entire club. Suddenly, friends of the "victim" swarmed in on Taylor and beat him unconscious. When Roger awoke in the hospital, he had stitches in his head and had suffered a concussion—from which he fortunately made a speedy recovery. The band, however, was deeply shaken by the incident and realized that their security would have to be an ongoing concern from now on. And poor Roger, never much of a crowd-hopper, decided to limit his public exposure even more.

Forging ahead despite this upsetting encounter, Duran Duran eagerly began their only British tour of 1982—twenty-four dates throughout the country between October 30 and November 27. The home front was anxiously waiting to see them. When the single "Rio" was released on November 1, it entered the national charts just shy of the Top 10, and shortly reached the number-nine slot—not bad for the album's fourth single. With satisfaction, the group watched as every date on the tour sold out, including six nights at London's Hammersmith Odeon and three more at their local Odeon in Birmingham. Saxophonist Andy Hamilton joined the lineup on the road, and one of the London audiences was given a special treat. Cockney Rebel leader Steve Harley, one of Duran Duran's musical heroes of the 1970s, joined them onstage and sang his anthem, "Come Up and See Me (Make Me Smile)." (Though Duran Duran haven't recorded other people's material, except for David Bowie's "Fame," they have on occasion encored with a band favorite, such as the Harley tune or Donna Summer's "I Feel Love.")

If there had ever been any doubt of how far Duran Duran would rise in their bid for stardom, the autumn 1982 English tour washed them away. Twenty years had passed since the Beatles had begun their supersonic rise from local Liverpool legends to a national—then global—phenomenon. Now, in 1982, the British press reported that Duran Duran were well on the way to following in that path. Daily newspapers such as the

London Star, never much for subtlety, blazed banner headlines like "Fab Five Fever! In 1962, the Beatles drove them crazy...And in 1982, Duran Duran do the same." Pictures were published showing mobs of Durannies clustered around the group's stage door, all yearning to see and touch their five handsome heroes. Any journalist who had been perceptive enough to predict the band's huge success earlier was now giving him or herself a large pat on the back. "The hottest property in pop," one *Star* reporter enthused, as he catalogued the group's string of successes around the world.

The band weren't about to deny all those comparisons between themselves and the Beatles. Nick Rhodes has deadpanned that Duran Duran were going to make a movie and call it "Yelp"—ha-ha-ha. But everyone felt that the parallels had more to do with fan mania than music. While proud of the fact that they, too, wrote catchy pop songs, just like John Lennon and Paul McCartney, Duran Duran were under no illusion that a cultural revolution was about to happen because they topped the charts.

"Why us?" Simon responded when the Beatle question was raised. "Because we're five individuals for a start. We're not spotty [pimply], three-foot-tall hunchbacks, which gives us the image; the Beatles were good looking." Admitting that looks aren't everything, Le Bon said, "I think we are popular because we offer kids options."

Coping with the increasingly large numbers of fans did weigh heavily on the group. It seemed that each week brought a new clever story that some follower devised to meet her favorite band member. Just as the Beatles were pelted with jelly beans when one admitted liking the sweet, Simon was deluged with European chocolates after he confessed to enjoying them—not a wise idea, since Le Bon is always kidded by the band about his tendency to put on weight! "The stories they invent are fabulous," he recalled. "One girl phoned my house and said she was working for a real-estate agent and had some papers she wanted me to see urgently." That scheme even traveled across the Atlantic. One American fan—pretending to be a lawyer but making all sorts of bizarre spelling errors in her letter—wrote that she just *had* to contact John Taylor, because he stood to collect a great sum of money from some investments.

Unfortunately, not all the fan activity was quite so harmless. The band takes pains to point out that they don't want anyone to be hurt because of loyalty to Duran Duran. Frequently on the British tour, the band had to be taken away from a theater in a police van. They worry that younger, smaller fans might be crushed when a crowd closes in, and do suggest that fans try to control their hysteria—but it's often a losing battle, according to Simon. "Once a mob of them jumped on our car after a concert and we couldn't shift them. They blocked all the daylight. I've never felt so frightened. I don't like it when they pull my hair or my clothes, but I understand why they do it," Le Bon admitted. "They want contact with you." Within reason, Duran Duran have always tried to fulfill that desire, sometimes risking their own safety.

Valiantly carrying on with all the mayhem at home, Duran Duran had no idea that the American breakthrough which had been so elusive was about to come flooding in. MTV had started its astonishing rise as the cable-TV industry expanded, and made the exotic Duran Duran videos a highlight of their programming to an estimated eight million people. Then, refusing to give up, Capitol Records put the remixed David Kershenbaum-produced songs onto *Rio* and reserviced the album to radio stations. Did those highly resistant program directors suddenly uncork their ears? Who knows—except that within days, hundreds of stations that had never given the band a fair shake now couldn't broadcast Duran Duran's music often enough. Just before Thanksgiving, *Rio* was something like number 140 on the national charts. As Christmas drew near, the album—a whopping six months after its initial release—had jumped 120 spots, on its way to an eventual number six position and multi-platinum sales.

All that seemed lacking was a hit single. That problem was solved when the new, punchier version of "Hungry Like the Wolf" was released on December 3, and swiftly climbed to number three on the U.S. charts. Anywhere one traveled in America, the seductive moaning of the song's backing singer might suddenly be heard, demanding attention. The track was reissued at exactly the right moment: Radio stations which had thought their audiences only wanted to hear the umpty-millionth airing of Led Zeppelin, the Doors, and other "album-oriented-rock" music, discovered that their ratings dropped. More adventurous upstart stations who played new music were the hottest turn of the dial in town, and that's where Duran Duran belonged—with the force of the future, not the rehashing of the past.

Christmas this year would be a happy, if unusually hectic time for Duran Duran. Andy grabbed a few days at home with his new wife, while Simon traveled around Canada, incommunicado from the world.

However, instead of ringing in "Auld Lang Syne" from England, everyone took a break from merrymaking and flew back to New York. Then MTV, which had assumed such an important role in popularizing the group when they really needed it, invited Duran Duran to appear in their second annual New Year's Eve telecast, live from the Savoy Theater in midtown Manhattan. Four groups would take turns heralding in the New Year for each American time zone. It was fitting that Duran Duran, who had spent so much time entertaining New York, would be chosen to greet 1983 with the East Coast.

The band arrived in New York, eager to ring in 1983 with their American fans. They ran through a quick rehearsal and were cheerfully interviewed for *Entertainment Tonight*. The scene inside the Savoy was almost as wild as the Times Square mob outside. Several members of the Rolling Stones, Stray Cats, Go Gos, and Blondie—among an entire laundry list of pop stars—all rubbed elbows. MTV "veejay" Alan Hunter finally introduced the group to an estimated audience of eight million, and they breezed through an enthusiastic one-hour set, starting with "Rio." After the band played the reflective "Save a Prayer," they left the stage, and everyone counted down the final seconds of 1982.

As 1983 roared in to the clamor of cannons and a burst of confetti, Duran Duran raced back out and performed a four-song finale of "Hungry Like the Wolf," "Planet Earth," "Careless Memories," and "Girls on Film." Like Debbie Harry had said months earlier, the band was a hard act to follow. "Simply put, Duran Duran was there firstest with the mostest," was how one journalist rated the night's attractions.

With barely a moment's rest between January and December, the members of Duran Duran viewed 1982 as a year of great accomplishments, ones which they had earned by perpetual hard work and a steadily optimistic attitude. Deftly managing to keep the level of their writing and performing high, the group pleased fans as well as winning the grudging admiration of some formerly surly critics. Shortly before their Christmas break, Nick reflected to journalist Betty Page, "I feel one of the major reasons for our band's success is that we don't have times when somebody really does lose control of reality. We try to keep everything between ourselves on an easily comprehensible level and not fake, so you retain your own personality and ideas. If you keep that relaxed confidence, I don't feel you can lose control."

Rhodes then related that a girl had stopped him on the street and asked for an autograph. When he cracked a joke about what he was doing, she commented, "God, I didn't think you'd be this human!" Nick was taken aback for a moment, but then realized that her remark made him quite happy. "When people find out we're the way we are," he said, "it gives them even more feel for getting into what we're doing than if they thought we were a bunch of pompous, arrogant young superstars."

Duran Duran had become a major world rock group during 1982. Perhaps they wouldn't have to push themselves so very hard in the years to come, but everyone knew that any lapse in quality would never be tolerated by an increasingly demanding music audience. When asked what he believed the next year would bring, Simon answered, "A lot more work." And, he hinted tantalizingly, "a little bit more diversification." Believing that the lavish rock and roll dreams of the excessive years were long gone, Duran Duran would widen their own interests past the next hit song or sold-out date, and give themselves the rewards that come with unique projects of lasting quality. The year 1983 would bring changes of scope, as well as style.

AWARD-WINNING IMAGES: DURAN DURAN'S VIDEOS

"**V**ideo to us is like stereo was to Pink Floyd. It was new, it was just happening. And we saw we could do a lot with it." In those few well-put sentences, Nick Rhodes summed up one of Duran Duran's most valued keys to success, particularly in the way the band finally broke through America's concrete-hard wall of resistance. Although the group had become a respected, on-the-way-up, chart act in Britain and Europe from the start (with their first single release, "Planet Earth"), in America only the most aware club-goers knew who they were. After a half-dozen successful singles at home, Duran Duran were just one small part of the so-called synth-pop movement in the eyes of highly dubious U.S. rock radio programmers. In the tradition of all great innovators, the group realized that they would do best to bypass that "album-oriented-rock" stranglehold completely. Instead, trading on the visual orientation that came to them naturally, the band sold its rock style via television—and became trailblazers.

Expressing themselves through visual means was easy for the group. Having been trained as an actor, Simon Le Bon knew the importance of presenting a story with his entire body, not just his voice. As the band's lyric writer, Le Bon easily gravitated to creating narratives that included strong images, transferable to the screen. "I take video very seriously; I see it as an art form," Simon commented. "Most people see it (only) as a promotional device or as a medium for documentary.... Videos are the 'talking pictures' of today's music industry." Nick has been a follower of film since he was a boy, and it was an automatic progression for him, too, to become involved in the creation of videos. In that respect, Rhodes has something in common with a great many of his countrymen. Britain is perhaps the single largest market for videocassettes, in terms of its population, throughout the world. Yes, even more so than America. Because Britain has only four TV channels, which don't broadcast late at night, video consumers buy millions of tapes to help fill in those tubeless hours.

Coupled with Britain's enormous video market is its great tradition of rock video music. The Beatles filmed promotional video clips almost twenty years ago, so that when they were busy traveling all over the world the band could still make appearances— even by proxy—on the British countdown chart show "Top of the Pops." This became an ongoing trend, as many of the biggest "British Invasion" groups recorded videos for TV shows at home, in Europe, and eventually throughout America, where they turned up on the now-classic rock shows "Shindig" and "Hullabaloo." Duran Duran were just five of the millions of young English people who grew up watching those videos. Obviously, the spirit of fun, frolic, adventure, and imagination that pervaded the clips—especially those by the Beatles—left their imprint.

When the group took on its current lineup back in 1980, they had many serious meetings to come up with a plan for distinguishing Duran Duran from the pack, and video was always a part of it. "We made a very conscious decision about video years ago," Simon admitted. "We thought about all the different kinds of mediums and techniques that were available to us without getting too gimmicky. We thought about what we could use that would take music further down the road. And it occurred to us: Video! We did a lot for video and video did a lot for us," he said.

EMI Records' excitement about Duran Duran's entire concept gave the band official support for their scheme, which proved to be one extra nudge in the right direction. Recognizing the potential of a band who could promote themselves visually, as well as on disc and in concert, an EMI video executive stated, "Duran Duran are a worthwhile investment—the songs they write lend themselves to visual interpretation. Some groups will be victims of the video age if their material does not translate naturally into visuals—just like the early film stars who did not survive the advent of the talkies."

Though Duran Duran knew that they wanted to make videos, they weren't sure at first who to enlist as their directors. One thing the band knew it didn't want was the images to simply plod along in time with the beat, reflecting what was already there and not adding any depth. For their first three songs from *Duran Duran*, the group tried out three directors: Television advertising genius Russell Mulcahy, who directed "Planet Earth;" the *I-D* team of Terry Jones and Perry Haines, who made "Careless Memories;" and the highly respected duo of Kevin Godley and Lol Creme, who were responsible for the infamous "Girls on Film" video. All were done in London.

Russell Mulcahy's imagination and flair came to light on the first of what would be his ongoing relationship with Duran Duran's videos. "Planet Earth" was a startling debut, with a science-fiction attitude, playing off the latest technology against some stylized battle scenes. Though the band were in their earliest, frilled-up costumes, Mulcahy's ability with flash cutting and special effects made the piece seem less dated than it otherwise might have become. "Careless Memories" did not fare as well, though its simple white-and-red color scheme was appealing. The band were less than thrilled with the somewhat stilted performance in this sequence, as the *I-D* direction seemed to value rather icy posing above emotional substance.

"Girls on Film" however, did spread the band's name around, both in positive and negative directions, and became somewhat legendary whenever it was shown on the American late night dance club circuit. However, after Duran Duran had completed work on their second album, *Rio*, they decided to avoid any more cheap shots and mature their visual horizons. A somewhat transitional video for "My Own Way," using an extreme red and black set, Spanish dancers, and a parrot, was directed by Russell Mulcahy, as a parting shot to London for a while.

Then, at enormous financial cost to the band (they were reimbursed by EMI after the money came out of their pockets), Duran Duran spent several months shooting five videos in Sri Lanka and Antigua, all directed by Russell Mulcahy. These brilliant images: "Hungry Like the Wolf," "Lonely in Your Nightmare," "Save a Prayer," "Rio," and "Night Boat" were impossible to confuse with just any old film clips. Simon's intricate, somewhat obscure lyrics were matched to exotic landscapes in which the band intrigued with— what else?—beautiful women.

The band agrees that their videos really begin with Simon, and at that point, only the song is being created. "Our videos work so well because Simon writes lyrics in 3-D," said Nick. "The images he conjures are so good it's no problem for us. He's always written like that, even before we knew we were going to make videos." Once the song is done, Rhodes continued, Russell Mulcahy's considerable input is welcomed. The director is given an idea of the band's desires, including location, storyline, costumes, and told their feelings about a particular song. In return, Mulcahy presents his own viewpoint to the band, and the final image gradually evolves. So Nick has little patience with those who complained about the band's travels to remote locations for the sake of obtaining evocative videos. "For the amount of enjoyment it gives people, and the way it helps people understand more about the sentiments of a song, I think it's worth every penny," he said flatly.

Working in film seems to come effortlessly to Duran Duran. Obviously, their physical attractiveness is enhanced by lush foliage, brilliant sunsets, exotic women, and stylish clothing. But the band are all diehard movie fans, partial to either classic black and white films or the latest special-effect masterpieces, so it makes sense that they, too, would enjoy participating in similarly well-planned productions. Simon easily described the filming of "Night Boat," making direct references to other films. "We filmed some very dusty, rural scenes with the five of us sitting on this slipway . . . much the same feeling as *Summer of '42*. We added some natural dialogue, then a couple of us slipped into monologues. And it showed, as the night fell, how things got weirder and weirder, until you've got this ghost ship with zombies aboard, attacking members of the group."

Though the group had despaired of becoming successful in the States, watching both *Duran Duran* and *Rio* slip into obscurity, their remarkable island-based videos reversed the tide, thanks in no small part to MTV. A bold experiment when it was launched in 1981 by Warner-Amex as a round-the-clock music channel, MTV was constantly on the alert for interesting videos to fill up all those programming hours. In its first months, the station had such a dire need of product that sometimes bands with no U.S. record deal got their videos played—certainly faring better on the fledgling TV channel than they could hope to do on commercial radio. MTV's acquisitions staff became aware of Duran Duran's most recent work, realized that the group would definitely appeal to their largely teenage and young adult audiences, and played the group repeatedly. As

with Australia's Men at Work, Duran Duran's videos
brought the band their first mass-market popularity,
forcing radio stations to follow suit or be hopelessly
left out in the cold.

Because MTV gave Duran Duran that all-important
exposure when they were on the verge of being dismissed as fly-by-nights, the band has in return given
the station its loyalty, with the rewards that entails.
The group flew to America specifically to appear on
the 1982 MTV New Year's Eve concert, which has
since been rebroadcast several times. Various members of the group have happily sat in as "veejays" on
the station, announcing videos of other artists and talking about their favorite performers. Perhaps most im-
portantly for the industry, Duran Duran have at times
given MTV a new song, such as "Union of the Snake,"
before handing it to the radio—who now, of course,
can't wait to get their hands on the group's latest material. To Nick Rhodes, this type of favoritism is fair
and just.

"The fact is, we didn't just come out of anywhere.
We toured America twice, long tours," he reflected.
"The radio stations weren't even interested in playing
one track off our album. Suddenly, MTV came across
several of our videos, and because they have a certain
amount of leeway, they decided they could actually
play one. Once we got the exposure, there were a lot
of letters coming in to MTV.... When we were finally
on heavy rotation with 'Hungry Like the Wolf,' it was
only then that the radio stations decided to change their
programming format to match that of MTV, and only
then that they decided we were good enough to be
played on their stations."

As MTV grew in importance, it would always eagerly premiere new videos by Duran Duran, and the
band obliged by keeping them coming. Ian Emes directed a black-and-white fantasy video for "The Chauffeur," which took the unusual step of not having the

group appear in it at all. Then, as the most recent inclusion on the band's first video album, it was back to London with Russell Mulcahy for the very modern "Is There Something I Should Know?" In this engaging video—starkly different from all the island pieces— the band's electric blue shirts contrast with a sinister set of spy-vs.-spy images, filmed around London's financial district and in local parks. Done with far less hoopla than the Sri Lanka and Antigua numbers, this compelling sequence reinforced the growing opinion that the band's music could be interpreted right in their own backyard with equal insight.

Simon vividly remembered filming that video, because on the same day, the band had to switch gears in midstream and do some London-based sequences needed for "Lonely in Your Nightmare." The result was a day which began with a five A.M. wakeup call at Le Bon's London hotel, six A.M. make-up session in the filmmaker's offices, and a cold day of filming, waiting, lunchbreak, more filming, lasting until eleven at night, when an exhausted Simon traipsed back home to his parents' house in Pinner. The results of all that exertion? For one, Duran Duran cleaned up at the video Grammy Awards, winning primarily for "Hungry Like the Wolf," a comfort to the band since their musical talents have not as yet led to receiving the coveted statuette.

Following the best-selling videocassette album released in March, 1983, the group have been more sparing with their videos over the past year, waiting until October to film "Union of the Snake"—a fire-and-brimstone adventure tale, in the style of *Raiders of the Lost Ark*, with Simon Milne directing. Then it was on to France in January for an appropriately "revolutionary" interpretation of "New Moon on Monday," complete with stampeding horses, befuddled villagers, and fireworks lighting up the wintry sky. The film has a bit of French dialogue preceding the action, cut down from an overly ambitious enterprise, which had been over twelve minutes long.

Only now, after they've traveled the world in search of the most exotic locations, have Duran Duran settled upon a more conventional in-concert presentation for their second video album. "The Reflex," filmed in Toronto during the 1984 world tour, is a tantalizing hint of the full-length performance cassette which the band released in October. John Taylor recalled how pleased the group was to have Russell Mulcahy back in charge of things, since he seems faultlessly able to capture and recreate the group's ideas. "Basically, the brief from us was that 'The Reflex' not only had to be a live video, but that it also had to be a live Duran Duran video, and that means it had to have certain stylizations—you know, like the the split-screen effect, that slightly conceptual feel, and so on. And it had to be stunning."

On Sunday, March 4, the concert at Maple Leaf Gardens was filmed. Then, the following day, with a show to do later at night, Mulcahy recorded closeups and special effects. From nine A.M. when they started, it was close to seven P.M. before the group finished— and had just enough time to shower and change into their next night's stage clothes. But the results had the unique effects Taylor hoped for: One can only imagine how compelling a full-length video done by such skilled hands will turn out. Duran Duran have won their reputation as video innovators, and it is perhaps the title of which they are proudest.

THE YEAR OF
LIVING ROYALLY

*T*he band needed time off. Well, at least some of them did. After a year of almost continual travel, Duran Duran decided to temporarily cut back on touring during 1983. Instead they planned to put together a serious video project, record a new LP without feeling rushed, and examine whatever else came along. They should have known that all manner of tempting offers would be made...but in January, everybody tried to relax by visiting at home and taking care of personal priorities. John Taylor finally found the time to decorate the flat in Birmingham which he had bought the year before. John was also asked to play on a session with Thin Lizzy's Scott Gorham. Andy, the other homebody, spent his days happily furnishing the lovely home he and Tracey shared—which he'd hardly slept in since the wedding!

On the other hand, workaholic Nick Rhodes had discovered an unknown band called Kajagoogoo and co-produced their debut single, "Too Shy," with Colin Thurston. Little did Rhodes imagine that his young finds would top the British singles charts before Duran Duran managed to do so. Nick had met the group's lead singer, Limahl, in London's plush Embassy Club and was reminded of how Duran Duran had behaved when they started out. "He knew what he wanted to do, and didn't care about anything else. He was really forward, you know, and he looked like a skunk, which couldn't be bad!" Nick laughed. When Nick took Limahl's tape to EMI Records, they immediately signed his band. Rhodes watched "Too Shy" soar straight to number one in February.

Of course, Nick and his fellow band members really didn't have to fear newcomers—or anybody else, for that matter. On February 9, Duran Duran cleaned up when the British Rock and Pop Awards were presented at London's Lyceum. Winning a third of the total votes cast, Duran Duran swept to the top of the "Best Group" category, and the "Best Album" listing, for *Rio*. Over twenty percent of voters cast their ballots for Simon Le Bon as "Best Male Singer," placing him comfortably on top there. Ironically, the only major category Duran Duran didn't win was "Best Single," because the votes had been divided between second place "Save a Prayer," fourth place "Rio," and "Hungry Like the Wolf."

Simon and Nick met with British reporters right after the ceremonies, and their exhaustion from overwork was apparent to the veteran journalists. Le Bon was hard pressed to stay awake for the ten-minute interview, because he'd just done a nine-hour photo session, which had involved reapplying makeup six times. "Here, feel this," he said, clutching a hank of hair that was rock-hard from styling gel. "The glamorous idol of millions?" asked one sympathetic writer. "Dozing quietly in a T-shirt, jeans and old sneakers, the Duran Duran lead singer looks more like the boyfriend everyone has and wishes *he* was Simon Le Bon."

Slightly more alert, the apparently unstoppable Nick pointed out that the group has always been willing to pay the price in return for success—subordinating sleep, normal relationships, and home and family life to the band's needs. "You have these big ideas about being a star," he said. "You think it just happens that you get to a certain position, then it sort of roller-coasts from there: That you ride around in big cars, pick up girls, drink champagne, and the money just keeps coming in. But for two years now, we haven't stopped working—day in, day out. It's the only way to stay on top. If you don't make the grade, it's no one's fault but your own."

So Duran Duran again postponed having a decent rest and went into the studio with co-producers Ian Little—who had been recommended to them by Roxy Music guitarist Phil Manzanera—and Alex Sadkin. The result, which they called their "interlude single" between *Rio* and *Seven and the Ragged Tiger*, was the very danceable "Is There Something I Should Know?". Released in England on March 14, 1983, the song entered the British charts at number one, giving Duran Duran their very first chart-topping record at home. They hardly had time to savor that long-awaited success, however, because the group was asked to pay another promotional visit to America. This one would make those reports about "Fab Five Fever" as accurate for America as they had been everywhere else in the world.

Justifiably proud of their eye-catching videos, Duran Duran readied their first video album, consisting of eleven songs, for release on a worldwide basis in March. As a way of launching what they hoped would be an ongoing series, the Sony corporation planned to issue two Duran Duran songs, "Hungry Like the Wolf" and the R-rated "Girls on Film," as a video single. Running shorter and less expensive than full-length cassettes, the singles would potentially appeal to those many people who had originally bought the group's records on audio disc.

Sensing the building hysteria about the band in Britain, and excited about their increasing exposure on MTV and radio in the States, Capitol Records executives booked Duran Duran on NBC's popular weekend series, "Saturday Night Live," and flew in the group ahead of time to build up steam. One ploy, which didn't work very well and was really a bit tacky, was repeatedly broadcasting the band's arrival time at JFK airport on Pan Am's Flight #1 over local radio stations and MTV. Instead of a zillion screaming fans—that would have come, but in another place, another time—less than a hundred stalwart followers showed up, hardly enough to tip over even one police barricade. The photographers went home disappointed, having clicked off just a few hasty snaps of five jet-lagged pop stars, calmly waving to the peaceable public.

A couple of days later, however, the situation was quite different. Advertisements appeared to come meet Duran Duran and have them sign a copy of the video single. The site chosen, Video Shack at Broadway and Forty-ninth Street in Manhattan, seemed perfectly suited to the event. The Times Square area in New York is accustomed to crowds congregating, and many in-person appearances had been held in nearby stores. By sunrise, though, fans were already lined up way down the block—many had traveled from the far suburbs in order to see the group up close. Thousands of people converged on the store which, imagining its doors, windows, and supply of cassettes—not to mention the band—crushed into splinters, asked for help from the police.

And they responded in droves, on foot and on horseback, waving clubs in the air to try and keep the increasingly hysterical crowd at bay. The screams of eager fans competed with police bull horns, making the scene appear close to a full-fledged riot. One of the event's publicists had been having trouble convincing hard-bitten TV news crews that Duran Duran's appearance was worth covering. Safely inside but watching the tumult escalate, she dialed all the stations again. "You want news?" she asked the assigning editors, then stuck the phone up to the windows. In a matter of minutes, every television station in New York City wanted to report about the three to five thousand people in the throes of Duranmania! Unfortunately, because conditions in the area had become dangerous for the group as well as the fans, very few people actually got to meet any of Duran Duran that day.

From that time on, everywhere Duran Duran turned up, groups of screaming girls would be waiting for them. The NBC building in Rockefeller Center, where "Saturday Night Live" is broadcast, was a favorite spot, because the group was obliged to spend many hours there rehearsing for the show. While the guards worried about their musical guests being torn limb from limb, Duran Duran happily cavorted inside. Growing impatient to practice their segments, the band started to play take offs of Rolling Stones and Billy Joel songs so loudly that a brawny stagehand warned Andy and Nick to cool it! Their part completed, the band could have elected to leave quietly through a side door, evading the teeming fans. But that's never been Duran Duran's style, and they boldly plunged into the crowd, signing as many autographs as possible and obediently smiling, smiling, smiling as the bulbs of a hundred Instamatics flashed in their faces. As Nick acknowledged during the midst of this chaotic time, "Because of the sort of people we are, we're very outgoing; it's very easy for us to accept that sort of thing. I like talking to people. I think as long as you're yourself, you don't become arrogant and you don't become nervous, as long as your personality doesn't change, you can take things like that in your stride.

"The only thing that does irritate me," he cautioned, "is when people rip clothes, rip buttons and things off of clothes, because you know how hard it is to replace things that are on jackets, or one-of-a-kind. That sometimes gets irritating, but it doesn't happen very often." John pointed out another reason for the band's empathy with their fans that many older groups might have put behind them long ago. "You have to remember that we are only just out of adolescence ourselves," he said to *TV Times*. "When I see a kid stand outside a hotel in the rain for twelve hours, I can sympathize. Only five years ago, I'd have done the same for Bryan Ferry."

Duran Duran would not formally return to the States for almost a year, as it turned out. They had, in those few chaotic days of zooming around town, given America a lot to remember them by. In the weeks to come, Capitol Records hit upon the idea of revitalizing the first Duran Duran album, which in 1981 had died a horrible death from inattention. They repackaged the LP with current photos of the band, and—those clever devils!—added "Is There Something I Should Know?" to the record, releasing it several weeks before the song's single version would be made available. This new and improved album started to sell like hotcakes, reaching number ten on the charts and ultimately reaching over a million buyers. In May and June, respectively, 7″ and 12″ singles of "Is There Something I Should Know?" followed the album into the charts. That small bit of vinyl would be all anyone would get from Duran Duran for almost another six months.

Their latest American adventure completed to everyone's satisfaction, Duran Duran returned home, where they realized it was time to start thinking about another album. By now, the group was sorely in need of a rest, and a stay in France seemed to be the answer to both problems. Obviously hoping that a good rest under the warm sun of southern France would spur their creative juices and restore their tired limbs to boyish bounciness, the five intrepid musicians left to spend almost three months on the Continent.

Just as Duran Duran had oriented themselves towards long work days in order to become successful, they now had to take a collective deep breath, stop chasing about, and learn how to relax. They booked into a beautiful chateau with spacious grounds on France's famed Côte d'Azur, and tried to interest themselves in its many facilities. Forever conscious about staying in shape, Simon frequently played tennis.

With the highly visible exception of Nick Rhodes, who emerged from the holiday as pale as he'd begun it, the band let themselves soak up very non-English tans.

When the Cannes Film Festival took over most of the neighboring coastal towns with thousands of deal-making movie moguls, the group wandered over. They were often photographed by the international press but found to their amazement that Duran Duran records were nowhere to be found in all of Cannes! Apparently, their fame had eluded this small corner of Europe, where to Nick's bemusement, Kajagoogoo's "Too Shy" was the most popular single of the entire year. Cannes also yielded up a choice selection of beautiful women, who leapt at the group's invitations to parties at the chateau. For a while, Simon's girlfriend Clare Stansfield and Nick's equally stunning model girl, American Julie Anne Friedman, kept their guys from growing too bored.

Within a couple of months, however, the band was yearning for the restless life, as they grew disappointed with themselves for not getting down to business concerning the next album. "Well, we were taking a lot of time out there," Nick admitted, shortly before recording was due to begin, "thinking about things, sorting things out.... It's all within," he laughed with a bit of embarrassment, obviously wondering how on earth they'd get a new album done when they were barely past having a title. According to Simon, someone had suddenly come up with the phrase, "the ragged tiger," and everyone responded to it. Various words were tacked on originally, including "running with the ragged tiger," until one band member suggested "seven and the ragged tiger," and they all felt that its somewhat mysterious connotations were just right for what the group was experiencing. It had an adventurous feel that was just right for all the exotic places the group had visited. "Piratey," said Simon. "Our direction is going to be a little different, a different mood," predicted Nick. "The first two were called good dance

albums by a lot of people, but the third is what *we* will
call a dance album," he prophesized with a gleam in
his eyes.

Early in June, a crew from the British television
station Channel Four visited Duran Duran in France,
and filmed them to star in a five-hour rock special
called "A Midsummer Night's Tube." Original Squeeze
member Jools Holland, now a well-known pop show
host in his own right, did the interviewing, and the
band were glad of his company. Champagne flowed
and fine food was served up upon request, as the band
admitted the isolation was driving them a little bats.
"I'm going crazy!" John told a reporter. "You can take
so much of this resting." "It's boring here," Andy remarked. "I've watched the same videos 'til I know
them by heart." Even though Roger's quiet nature made
him appreciate the peace and quiet, he, too, felt ready
to get back to work. Simon summed up their feelings
with typical honesty: "I suppose we miss being famous."

Once the filming was completed—following the usual
mishaps and an argument when the band didn't like
some of Holland's questions—everyone's good nature
was restored. Deciding it was the enforced laziness
that had made them short-tempered, Duran Duran
hopped on a plane along with the TV crew and headed
for home three weeks ahead of schedule. "If that's how
millionaires live, they can keep it," declared John, having had quite enough of the aristocratic lifestyle. No
one argued with that!

It was time to record an album—no more fooling
around. In late June, Duran Duran flew to the Caribbean island of Montserrat to begin formal sessions for
Seven and the Ragged Tiger. Maybe it was foolish of
them to embark for another fairly remote location, considering how a couple of months in southern France
had affected their creative processes. But Duran Duran
knew that working at home would have been out of
the question. "We were getting to the stage where we

were regarded as public property," said a weary Andy Taylor.

Accompanied by management and the two co-producers, Alex Sadkin and Ian Little, the group caught successively smaller planes, and finally a stream of hired cars, that took them into the island's leafy hills, in which AIR Studios was tucked away—a lone hub of activity in the humid tropical heat. For five weeks, the band attempted to work on the album, as well as rehearse for a pair of prestigious charity performances they'd been asked to give back in England at the end of July. The locals were obviously used to having major pop music stars in their midst. Fan mail poured in from around the world, sometimes addressed "Duran Duran, West Indies"—yet somehow, the messages got through to the cluster of luxurious white villas, which the group called home.

Since it was opened five years ago by renowned Beatles producer George Martin, AIR Studios has been hired by many of the world's biggest acts, including the Police, Paul McCartney, Stevie Wonder, and Elton John. The location is tailor-made for performers to work in complete comfort with the most modern technology, but still be able to enjoy a good rest when they need it. Without nightclubs, discotheques, or nearby fashionable towns to distract them, Duran Duran got down to the basics of recording. Having learned a lot about studio work as a result of the two previous LPs, they were able to use their time more productively than ever before. Said Andy, in his typically straightforward manner, "This is probably the album we wanted to make first time round, but it takes a few to get it right."

Nick was a little more specific about their goals. "Exactly what do we want this to sound like? Let's not think about the last album at all; let's think this is the first album—which I think is the most positive attitude you can go in with to record your first, second, sixth, or nineteenth album." The group knew they were aiming for a dance record. So although all was well with the new producers, the group did have to make sure that Alex Sadkin didn't give their new record too much of the island rhythms he loved.

Never neglecting their fashion sense for a minute—no matter how remote the locale—Duran Duran included a wardrobe mistress amongst the service staff who tended the villas. Just as they follow their individual fashion dictates when the group performs, each member also dressed in a unique way for studio work. Simon, displaying his tanned form, wore pink shorts and a T-shirt. John preferred going barefoot much of the time and sported baggy black trousers, which had dozens of pockets in every conceivable place. Nick, not one to break character, always wore his makeup and tended to silk shirts, even in this sweat-inducing land. He never even left his villa until mid-afternoon and always stayed in the shade—the group's own version of Count Dracula! Roger, the opposite of Nick's lean pallor, browned his muscular body to a healthy glow by continual swimming in their choice of pools. Roger rarely even wore shirts at all during his island stay. And Andy, who let his hair grow so long his mates probably feared they'd soon lose him to a heavy metal band, looked like a Caribbean pirate of ages past. He tied his hair back into a generous tail and paraded around in loose-fitting shirts and cut-offs. What a merry crew they made, almost as colorful as the brilliantly flowered gardens and wildlife that populated the island.

No one expected these five globe-hoppers to work around the clock. Though the usual recreations of cities and crowds were far away, the resourceful band found other ways to pass the time. Visits by Tracey Taylor, Julie Anne Friedman, and Clare Stansfield kept Andy, Nick, and Simon pretty content. John and Roger didn't want for company, either, as an array of beautiful girls always seemed to know where Duran Duran would be on any given day. Whenever any visitors arrived from home, they brought armfuls of new magazines featuring the group, and some impressive brochures from

London real-estate agents. About to become million-aires, several of the group hadn't even been able to find time in which to purchase a home.

The days passed pleasantly and routinely, at least when there weren't any ear-shattering hurricane winds whipping around—it was that time of year. From morning until midday, the group's early risers explored and played at sports—swimming, sailing, surfing, and riding around the narrow, winding mountain roads—sometimes quite perilously, as John found out once when his brakes failed. Eventually, by afternoon, they'd trickle into the studio and work long hours, into the night. If friends were around, the only chance they'd have for socializing was during dinner break, which was eaten on a balcony above the studio. Then it would be more work for the group, and American television via satellite, pingpong or billiards for visitors until, hours later, Duran Duran would emerge and start to wind down. John instituted middle-of-the-night pop-music quizzes, with the losers ending up in the pool at four A.M.

Not a bad life at all, an observer would think—and at least one pair of fans was determined to be part of it. Two twenty-four-year-old British nurses saved almost two thousand dollars each to fly to Montserrat and stay for two weeks. Every day, they waited outside the studio for a chance to have a quick chat with the group. Knowing the true value of loyalty, the group invited these two lucky ladies to dinner and gave them signed autographs. The girls agreed that it was worth the wait, and the expense.

There were a few setbacks owing to ill-health, which put a damper on the group's spirit of adventure. Too much windsurfing resulted in Roger getting a bad case of sunstroke. Much more serious, though, was Nick's condition. Since he wasn't at all suited to life in the tropics, Nick was plagued by food poisoning and was advised to take vitamins. Because of his inability to withstand the sun, he kept indoors most of the day.

On one occasion, Rhodes suddenly stopped cold in the midst of recording; to everyone's horror, his heart was racing and he was talking incoherently! The keyboardist was flown to see a doctor in Miami, who told Nick he had something called paroxsymal tachycardia, which causes the heart to beat double time. Nick was informed that it resulted from overwork and was advised to slow down. However, for him, the best medicine would be to leave the West Indies and get back to rainy old England.

What did draw the band away from the tropics and back to their wet homeland—only four days after Duran Duran officially marked their third anniversary together—was an invitation they couldn't refuse: Royalty! Duran Duran were among several popular bands asked by Prince Charles and Princess Diana to perform at the Prince's Trust charity concert in London. Never mind that the group would be surpassed as headliners by more established artists Dire Straits—they knew who the most exuberant audiences would be cheering for. And three days later, there was another charity function they wished to appear at—this one at the Aston Villa Football Ground, at home in Birmingham. There, Duran Duran would receive full headline billing—as if anyone would try to presume differently. Between the two shows, almost one-half million dollars was anticipated being raised for the charities.

Once the bookings were confirmed, the band quickly switched gears and rehearsed, practice including several of the songs written for their new album. Naturally, everyone was looking forward to these prestigious shows, although reactions within the group ranged from Nick's prediction that "we're going to have an alarmingly splendid occasion," to Andy's hope that the Prince might even "mildly perspire." As for nerves, John declared that he wouldn't be as nervous meeting Charles and Diana as he was when he first met David Bowie! Andy, however, was already hearing from his delighted relatives up north and acknowledged that he for one was a little weak-kneed anticipating the event. "It's something to tell your kids and grandchildren about because Prince Charles and Princess Diana will be the King and Queen, and the King and Queen of England's still the *King and Queen of England*, no matter what anybody says," he loyally declared.

"Durandemonium," the London *Daily Express* bannered its headline, reporting about the hundreds (some said thousands) of fans who swarmed Heathrow Airport and loudly welcomed their favorite group back home. Comparisons to the Beatlemania of the 1960s were everywhere, and Duran Duran were tagged all over the country as "The Fab Five." Simon, accompanied by Clare Stansfield, tried to be calm about it all, as he dodged questions about his romance. Barely escaping the fervent clutches of the crowd, the group ducked into a "getaway car," and headed for their luxurious rooms in the Grosvenor House Hotel.

That car ride into town was about the only relative peace that Duran Duran would have during their entire week at home. Jet-lagged and sleepy, the band nevertheless did a quick clothes change, put on a little street makeup, and obligingly posed for dozens of news photographers. "We're just this week's story," said Simon, trying to keep it all in perspective. "Next week, it'll be something else."

July 20, 1983, was the day when Duran Duran truly crossed the boundary from a very successful pop group, and became household words. "Everybody recognized me, everybody was aware—not just the kids," said an astonished John Taylor, as he recalled that very special show's aftermath. Ironically, due to the group's prolonged absence from the road, the royal performance was not one of their best sets. Numerous technical problems, including two broken drum pedals and snapping strings, marred the forty-five-minute show for quality. It was a rough break, especially when the press made a big deal out of it following the show, but the group tried to take it in stride.

Besides, there was no doubting that the four thousand screaming fans who were lucky enough to be inside the Dominion Theatre, as well as the Royal couple, were very pleased that Duran Duran had given the show, problems or not. As Duran Duran drove up to the hall, they were greeted by the yells of more well-wishers, who had lined Tottenham Court Road and brought its usual busy traffic to a standstill. Before the set, the group not only had to contend with pre-show nerves, they were invited to meet England's future king and his beautiful young princess. The next day, newspapers around the world would repeat Charles and Diana's brief conversation with the band. The Princess asked if they'd been "rehearsing like mad." When Simon replied, "We have," Diana said sympathetically, "Then you must be exhausted. I don't envy you in this heat."

After Prince Charles publicly thanked Duran Duran for participating in the program—and received a howl of shrieks in return—he and the artists had a more relaxed opportunity to chat during at late evening reception. Duran Duran had been mentioned as one of the Princess' favorite musical performers, and Nick noted with pleasure that she and Prince Charles knew quite a lot about their recent recording activities. England's future monarch also confided to the group that he liked their clothes. "I rather like your gear," Charles said. "What do you call it?"

With Duran Duran and their royal admirers plastered on every front page in the British Isles, the three days until the band's grand homecoming concert flew by. The band booked into Birmingham's local Holiday Inn, and the hotel was immediately ringed by fans, screaming, "Come to the window, Simon!" (Fill in your favorite—no one was left out). Three enterprising girls saved up fifty dollars and reserved rooms inside, the better to luck into a personal encounter with the band.

One young girl found herself in the group's company by their invitation, and couldn't believe it was real.

Ellen Hanslow, fourteen, had been tragically orphaned only a week earlier, when her parents were among twenty people killed in a helicopter crash. Learning of the girl's dreadful experience, Duran Duran generously included her in their Birmingham concert, complete with an in-person meeting at their hotel. Blushing from Roger and Simon's good luck kisses, the brave girl thanked the band for bringing something good into her life. Simon spoke for everyone when he softly said, "It was the least we could do."

Duran Duran's benefit concert in aid of MENCAP (a mental illness relief organization) was as wonderful as anyone could have hoped. John and Roger remembered that the last time they'd set foot in their local football stadium, they got chased away by Scottish supporters of a rival team. Today, however, the field was all theirs. Even a rainstorm, which had Simon shaking his fist at the grey sky, had ended by afternoon. As the clouds lifted, the crowd poured in—twenty thousand in all—who listened politely to openers Prince Charles and the City Beat Band, and then Robert Palmer, but saved their loudest cheers until eight-thirty, when a black curtain parted to reveal Birmingham's local heroes.

Reviewers agreed that this show had none of the flaws of the royal performance. Simon raced across the stage at a frantic pace, propelling an audience that didn't need any encouragement to simply go wild. "Union of the Snake" was performed live for the first time, and its encouraging reception told the band they were heading in the right direction with their latest recordings. And for those who didn't think Duran Duran were likely to explore new directions, the band played a ferocious version of Iggy Pop's "Funtime," which caught the critics off-guard. There could only be one place suitable for an after-show party and, indeed, Duran Duran celebrated the night away at the Rum Runner. Everyone was happy and more relaxed than they'd been in months, success on a grand scale being the best possible reward for hard work.

Before they bid an all-too-hasty farewell to Britain for what would be another five months, Duran Duran gave one final piece of news to the home folks. Lead singer Simon Le Bon, focus of a huge chunk of attention within the group, had proposed marriage to model Clare Stansfield, and she had accepted. Simon gifted his fiancée with a white-gold and diamond ring, and Clare confided the romantic story of how she and Le Bon had fallen in love to the newspapers. So unlike Andy and Tracey Wilson-Taylor's homegrown courtship, Clare had gone to a Duran Duran concert at her home in Toronto, but spent the whole set chatting with friends in the bar. When the girls happened to run into the group at another bar later, Clare asked Simon, "What do you do?"—she didn't even recognize him!

Simon was immediately entranced by the young model and invited her to a party that night. Clare turned him down, as they'd only just met. The band flew off to continue their 1982 American tour, and Simon began to phone Clare from every city they were in. The couple didn't spend any real time together until Clare flew to Montserrat, only to pass her time alone, sunbathing, while Simon worked long hours in the studio. In the end, their affection for one another surmounted the difficulties of spending time together, and Clare decided that she was ready to face the wrath of Simon's fans as the future Mrs. Le Bon. Fortunately, most of the group's followers accepted Clare as they had done the year before when Andy married Tracey, and treated her with courtesy and kindness.

Some dooomsayers tried to imply that the group's popularity would decline as each member got married. They tried that with the Beatles, too, twenty years earlier, and it hadn't held water then, either. When asked about weighing their personal lives against the group's fame, Duran Duran took distinctly independent views, resenting the negative implications of outsiders and giving their supporters some credit. Said

Andy to *Melody Maker*, "For God's sake, you can't say to yourself, 'I can't get married because of what people might think.' I suppose it does flicker through your mind, though...(but) there's much more potential in having somebody you love than being on your own, especially in this business, because all you'd do is be out of your brains twenty-four hours a day, and then you'd get lost in the rock star thing.... It's good to tie yourself to somebody and keep the stability."

Roger expressed the very realistic—if not always easy to accept—point of view that, "If I wanted to get married tomorrow, I'd get married tomorrow. I just live my personal life exactly how I want to." Since Simon's engagement, Nick has come close to tying the knot with his American girlfriend, and both Roger and John have conducted long-term relationships (John with actress Janine Andrews for over three years), though these have been less-publicized romances. In fact, when Roger married his girlfriend of four years, dance instructor Giovanna Captone, this summer in Italy, the event came as a total surprise to the outside world. Simon was the drummer's best man. Hopefully, today's fans are mature enough not to demand that their heroes isolate themselves from the world, including true love.

Returning to Montserrat in late July, Duran Duran attempted to close up shop on *Seven and the Ragged Tiger*, but soon realized that the West Indian paradise had its limitations. The raw tapes of songs they'd created were fine, as far as they went, but no one felt comfortable locking themselves up again in semi-isolation. "We had to go somewhere there was life!" emphasized Nick, when it came time for the album to be mixed. Numerous suggestions were nixed: Nassau, because who needed to be stuck on yet another remote island; London, because they would have had to contend with fanmania and record company pressures; Los Angeles and New York, because too much nightlife would be just as bad for them as none at all.

Ultimately, Duran Duran decided to head clean over to the other side of the world, and finish the album in Sydney, Australia. The band had been to the Land Down Under once before, during their 1982 tour, and found quite a lively scene going on with lots of local talent, such as Men at Work. Add to the musical stimulation Australia's beautiful coastline beaches and lovely weather for water sports, and it seemed an ideal compromise to the group. They checked into lavish apartments, but after an all-too-short five days of leisure, mixing sessions began in earnest and eighteen-hour days in the studio were not uncommon. Once, the band even invited several loyal fans inside EMI Studios to sing background on a track. Unfortunately, after working for days on what would have been the LP's title song, "Seven and the Ragged Tiger" was eventually scrapped by the group in favor of "The Seventh Stranger."

After more than two months spent in mixing, the album was completed at last, and not a moment too soon for the five exhausted musicians. Nick expressed the band's overall feeling that working on one record for over six months was a frustrating experience, though the end result was an album everyone would take pride in. "When you spend so much time on a project, you go through stages," he recalled. "You wonder if you're going in the right direction, or whether what you've already got is right or how much longer it's going to take or whether it's better than what you've done before. After about four months, we'd scrapped so much material, we knew that what we'd kept was fairly positive for us."

The first test of *Seven and the Ragged Tiger*'s extraordinary pulling power came when "Union of the Snake" was released worldwide on October 17, 1983, as a 7″ and 12″ single. One after another surprised reviewer bowed to Duran Duran's newfound sophistication, and praised the band for their highly accomplished instrumental skills—said with an awe appropriate to their relative youth and inexperience. Before long, the chart figures spoke for themselves: "Union of the Snake" went to number three in Britain—a disappointment to the band because it didn't reach the top at home—but it did achieve the number-one slot in America, and everyone was thrilled about that. Things certainly appeared promising for the lengthy U.S. tour they would be undertaking early in 1984. An elaborate video, done with director Simon Milne, helped keep attention focused on the group. But Duran Duran's photo session for the LP cover was what really turned into a traffic stopper.

"It turned into a bit of a production number," John sheepishly admitted, and that doesn't say the half of it. Photographer Rebecca Blake and her crew were flown in from America and graphic designer Malcolm Garrett from England. When no tigers were available in Sydney, one was sent by private jet from Melbourne. The album cover shooting was done on the steps of Sydney's public library with band; makeup, and wardrobe personnel; TV crews; animal handlers—and a flood of local fans—all milling around. Somehow, after shot upon shot was taken and rejected, the album's startling cover was finally achieved, at a cost which was rumored to run to a six-figure sum. Notice that the band and the tiger appear on different parts of the sleeve—a wise idea, and one that certainly must have soothed the nerves of management and musicians alike!

Completion of the album took more time than expected, so Duran Duran had only ten days rehearsal before their next World Tour would begin. With a string of Australian dates coming up, John and Roger popped over to Japan for a promotional visit that would herald the group's arrival back in the Far East shortly after the New Year. The now-expected chaos and hysteria ensued in massive proportions. When they returned to Sydney, a rehearsal hall was hired, and the set was hammered together with startling efficiency. Even without an audience, Simon and Andy were almost uncontrollable as they bounded all over a makeshift stage. Patiently, the guest musicians for the tour, American saxophonist Scott Page, percussionist Raphael de Jesus, and backup singers B.J. Nelson and Charmaine Burch, were put through their paces. Rattling about the near-empty room, with silence greeting the end of every number, the band imagined in their minds the way in which arenas around the world would resound when they set out on the road.

As Duran Duran launched the Australian segment of their world tour, *Seven and the Ragged Tiger* was released around the world on November 21, 1983. In the United States, it shipped gold and entered the chart in the Top 30, the swiftest climb any of the band's LPs had ever made. The ecstatic Australian response throughout Duran Duran's tour hinted at the kind of extreme reactions they would draw in the months to come. Performing before crowds that ranged up to twelve thousand in size—an impressive amount for the relatively sparsely populated land, the group was greeted with wildness that remained front-page news. In Melbourne, when the band appeared on their stage set with Roman-style columns, one newspaper reported, "Certainly, by the end of the night, the concert seemed to be a lions and Christians contest, the lions being about five thousand screaming teenagers."

Reports of Duranmania from abroad were filtering around the world, as young people in many nations started counting down the days before the group would be visiting their cities. In America, where almost eighteen months had passed since the band's last tour, excitement was at fever pitch. Before they barreled through America, however, Duran Duran were going back home to Britain for Christmas, and no sweeter place to finish out this wondrous year existed for them. "I've never been so homesick in my life," said Simon, surveying yet another teeming crowd who welcomed Duran Duran at Heathrow.

AT HOME
AROUND THE
WORLD

*N*o sooner were the British Duran Duran tour dates announced than they sold out, usually within hours. Four extra shows were quickly added onto the tour, which began December 6 at the Manchester Apollo and culminated just before Christmas with five nights in London's arena-sized Wembley Stadium. Money carefully saved up for holiday gifts instead found its way to box offices all over Britain. For fans who had waited an entire year to see Duran Duran appear in a full-scale series of shows, $10 was a very reasonable price to pay. And when several of the shows immediately sold out, bus packages were offered to those willing to travel to nearby cities rather than miss seeing the spectacle altogether.

With the Australian tour having served as a high pressure warmup for the home crowds, Duran Duran didn't disappoint the hundred thousand or so fans who saw them perform in Britain. Their column and pillar stage set was the group's most elaborate backdrop ever, and video screens hanging from the ceiling made it possible for even those relegated to back rows to catch every nuance of each song. In tribute to the warm reception given them in the Land Down Under, Duran Duran returned the favor by enlisting the band Australian Crawl as their opening act. The expanded lineup they had used earlier for the two charity shows reappeared on this world tour: sax player Andy Hamilton, percussionist Rafael de Jesus, and vocalists B. J. and Charmaine helping the group to fill every corner of Britain's biggest theaters.

Opening night in Manchester typified the frenzy into which Duran Duran threw their homeland. Fans by the hundreds dressed in favorite bits of band gear, including buttons, T-shirts, scarves, John Taylor-style fedoras—even terrycloth wrist bands with Duran Duran printed on them, in the fashion of Simon's athletic gear. Out in the lobby, excited members of the crowd parted with cash in return for a staggering array of Duran Duran collectibles: programs, posters, more buttons, sweatshirts—it was possible to dress head to toe in Durania.

As the lights dimmed, any stragglers quickly dived into their seats, and two thousand screaming voices almost drowned out the opening instrumental, "Tiger Tiger." For the next ninety minutes, the excitement was nonstop, all the way from "Is There Something I Should Know?" through a second encore of "Girls on Film." The tour was carefully designed to showcase many of the band's newest numbers, with "The Reflex" and "New Moon on Monday" being received so ecstatically that their future success as singles was a fait accompli. Of course, the band didn't neglect either of their earlier albums, and included a representative cross-section of oldies, such as "My Own Way" and "Save a Prayer." At one point in the proceedings, Simon's acting background must have got the better of him, and he began a long, involved introduction which questioned, "Did you ever get the feeling when you were walking alone at night, that you were being followed?" All that was missing was a monster to jump out of the bushes! John and Andy, deciding that Simon had better cut out the monologue, immediately began to unmercifully tease the singer. After begging the guitarists to let him be serious—with no luck—Simon got back to business, launching into "Cracks in the Pavement."

Always fashion conscious, Duran Duran had acquired some interesting new clothes for the tour. John wore black, complemented by a plaid scarf thrown over one shoulder. Andy dressed all in white, including a white hat and even a headband, to restrain his increasingly long locks. Roger was the most casually clad, fitted out in a blue pullover and white trousers. Nick, his hair dyed once again to a fire engine red, elegantly played up contrasts with a blue suit and white shirt. Finally Simon, slimmer than he'd been in a while, highlighted his trim contours with a brilliantly designed pullover and tight black trousers. The total impact was devastating, and the audience responded by throwing a sea of presents onto the stage—keeping tour associate Simon Cook busy clearing it off, so that perpetually active Simon Le Bon wouldn't stumble on a stuffed animal, or for that matter, a bit of silky underwear. As one daily newspaper accurately predicted, observing the opening show, "If this first night of their world tour was anything to go by, Duranmania is about to take the country by storm once more."

As the tour hurtled on, the band traveling between cities in an elaborately outfitted coach, screaming hysteria hallmarked every show. Having decided to accept Andy's wife Tracey as part of the Duran Duran entourage, fans weren't always so forgiving about Simon's Clare or Nick's Julie Anne. "It's all perfectly normal," said Rhodes with understanding. "Andy's married, and when the rest of us decide to settle down, we'll let people know." However, on those occasions when any of the band's parents were spotted by the eagle-eyed crowd, they were treated respectfully, almost with awe, as if they'd brought up gods, not talented flesh-and-blood young men.

If there was any show the band anticipated more than their five sold out Wembley concerts, it was homecoming night at the vast modern National Exhibition Centre, just outside Birmingham. Those 11,500 people waiting inside—with another show, just as large, the next day—meant a great deal to Duran Duran, and the group hoped that the people who had started out with them years ago would still be happy.

They needn't have worried. Birmingham remained true to its conquering heroes, even if some unusual moments did occur. Those oh-so-tight trousers gave Simon a bit of trouble, several buttons popping off in the middle of the set. Like a flash, Le Bon vaulted over to the side of the stage, where the damage was quickly repaired by a seamstress. And with a *Rolling Stone* reporter along to document the night, the entire world was soon informed that Simon Le Bon wore blue underwear. Far more enjoyable to the singer was a chance to see an old school chum after the show. Simon hadn't seen his friend from Pinner, Claire Sheraton, for twelve years, and the twosome happily recalled hanging out in her house, playing Rolling Stones records. "I wasn't surprised he became a star. He was always very dramatic," said Claire. "He was always easy to talk to and still is."

Of course, Duran Duran's five-night stint at Wembley Stadium, for each of which they drew in 28,000 people, was the most visible sign of their superstardom. Typically, the music press writers gave the band a hard time, while their fans pretty much agreed with one overwhelmed 16-year-old who said, "This is what it must be like to die and go to heaven." The group tried to keep their perspective somewhere in the middle, staying strictly down to earth. For all the glamour which surrounds the band's image, one reporter pointed out that Duran Duran were paying over $100,000 per week to keep the show on the road, had three-quarters of a million dollars tied up in lights and sound equipment, and were not yet, in fact, millionaires. (They certainly have reached that magic figure by now, thanks to their American tour and most recent two best-selling singles.)

Simon Le Bon, who as frontman is always the most visibly pressured in the group, developed his own method of coping with such incredible stress, and practiced it throughout the tour. "I psyche myself up for an hour and need to be left alone. After a sound check, I go back to the hotel and I won't talk to anybody. People might think it's unsociable," Simon realized, "but it has to be like that. I have a bath, read a bit, or watch television. Then I do some voice exercises. I deliberately starve myself of communicating, so that when it comes to walking onstage, I really feel like getting something over." As long as Duran Duran assume that degree of care and concern for their audiences, the message will come through, loud and clear.

The tour took a temporary breather for a very happy Christmas to be celebrated with family and loved ones, since the mad rush of activity was scheduled to resume almost immediately after the New Year. And things did begin to happen right away, with the single of "New Moon on Monday" being released in America on January 3, 1984, and quickly soaring up the international charts, eventually reaching number ten in the States. By the time the record was issued to the British market two weeks later, the band had already traveled to France where, for a change, they had an unspoiled good time shooting a video.

Not having either the time or inclination to scout anywhere particularly exotic for the "New Moon on Monday" filming, the band joyfully opted to work in the French countryside. They settled themselves into a village about 150 miles south of Paris, called Noyes, and worked with the entire town's cooperation. "The Mayor thought it was brilliant," laughed John. What emerged was three times longer than the song's four minutes—a whole short story captured on film. At one stage, the band even had some dialogue in it, though that ended up on the cutting room floor because of time limitations.

From France, it was on to Japan until the end of January, where the band not only thrilled many thousands of their Far Eastern fans, but caused the very

earth to move! Just kidding—what actually happened
was that the group, many of their crew and entourage
were trapped on the twenty-fourth floor of a hotel when
Japan was hit with an earthquake, a frequent occurrence. No serious damage occurred, except possibly
to the band's understandably sensitive nervous sys-
tems.

Anyway, Duran Duran could certainly shake off any
fears if they turned an eye towards America, where
tour preparations were being made at a fevered pitch.
The band's most extensive U.S. schedule of concerts
to date was set to kick off February in Seattle. Originally planned to comprise thirty cities, representatives
of the group soon figured out that extra shows would
have to be added, so great was the crush for tickets.
In addition to the two Madison Square Garden dates
in New York, Duran Duran's appearances in Los Angeles, Detroit, Cleveland, and Chicago also sold out
within hours of being announced. Soon those treasured
seats, ranging in price from $11 to $16, were being
scalped for up to $160 each.

Many fans from cities that were not included on the
route decided they had to change the band's mind, and
did something about it. About 83,500 signatures were
placed on petitions in San Francisco and San Diego,
demanding appearances by Duran Duran in those cities. Eventually, the tour was lengthened so much that
the group remained in America for almost two and a
half months, not returning to England until mid-April.

While no one had planned to be away from home
for such a long time, considering the amount of traveling they'd just completed in 1983, America's dedication to Duran Duran was a fact that none of the band
would ignore. "Britain has never been one to celebrate
its heroes, unlike America," John remarked, and after
having worked so hard to become successful, the band
quite honestly wanted their achievements to be appreciated. Always maintaining that Duran Duran had

wanted from the start to play the world's largest venues, this was their golden opportunity to do so.

The cold winter of 1984 unfurled its blasts on the heart of America, as Duran Duran traveled across the country, spreading their own special kind of warmth. Seeing the dismal weather that greeted many of the late February dates in particular, Simon made a point of thanking fans for braving the elements and coming to the shows. In their own private jet (a necessity, with delayed commercial flights a frequent cold weather occurrence), the band played in cities from west to east— then reversed their course, to end in California on April 16. The entire tour was sponsored by Coca-Cola, whose logo was prominently displayed on tickets, ads for the show, and backdrops inside the halls.

Everywhere Duran Duran appeared, reaction was the same—jaundiced critics not knowing quite what to do about arenas filled with thousands of screaming girls, hollering for a band who were very serious about the quality of their music. It seemed impossible for the two sides to ever mesh, but usually, by evening's end, Duran Duran had pulled some grudging respect out of the cynics, while satisfying their adherents from first note to last.

From the *Pittsburgh Press*: "The sound system, while plenty loud, brought Le Bon's voice through clearly. To have buried it would have been a disservice because he has a fine voice and uses it well."

From the *Detroit Free Press*: "Even the parents (of fans) complimented the group's melodic, danceable pop and its slick, clean image. Unlike so many rock bands pandering to the teen market, Duran carries a sense of innocence and romanticism. . . . The group's show was worth the price of admission, and it was certainly worth the fans' shouting about."

From the *Hartford Evening Sentinel*: "Some thirteen thousand howling, screaming adolescents drove to the state's capital city through one of the worst storms of the season, just judging from their reception of Simon Le Bon and his friends, the treacherous trip was well worth it."

From the *Washington Post*: "Duran Duran's music is improving noticeably. Having reached the mania level, the group could have put out almost anything and watched it go platinum. Instead, they spent one thousand hours in the studio and came up with an album, *Seven and the Ragged Tiger*, that's certainly not standard teen fare."

By the time Duran Duran arrived in New York for their two long awaited Madison Square Garden dates, the tour pattern had already established itself. Differing from their 1983 visit, when the band's itinerary was practically handed out to any fan who wanted it, this time the group was being a lot more cautious. For their own peace of mind, they moved in secrecy—escorted into limousines by hulking bodyguards, then speeded away into the night. Nick's two-room hotel suite had only one working telephone, which rang repeatedly every time Rhodes hung up the receiver. The phone by the bed had been torn out of the wall the previous night, he explained. Julie Anne couldn't take the non-stop hysteria and finally lost her temper.

"If we toured like this for the next ten years, I think we'd be complete morons," Andy admitted. "I don't think the human body or mind is built to do that. We get crank calls, so we've got to have a secret code to get through to our phones. It may sound stupid, but if someone is gonna call you in the middle of the night and wind you up, saying, 'I know where you're staying. I hate your band....'" The guitarist's voice lost its energy and tapered off in dismay. More than anything else, Andy missed having Tracey on the road with him. But, he elatedly added, the reason for her absence was that by late summer, Andy Taylor would become a father—and that was worth waiting for!

Trying valiantly to keep the hotel room destruction to a minimum, and not acquire one of those "awful group" reputations, Duran Duran fell back on their bizarre sense of humor to carry them over the long boring hours of waiting, coupled with a fishbowl existence. On one occasion, Simon decided to have a little wicked fun. He turned up for a soundcheck, arm in a sling, pretending to have slipped on the ice. Some of the band immediately wanted to shelve the performance, the crew tried to shift things around to accommodate a bandaged lead singer, and the promoter was on the verge of heart failure. Finally, two hours later, Andy innocently wondered how Le Bon planned to wave his hands in the air and get the audience to clap along, always a part of the show. "Like this!" Simon yelled, and threw off the sling. Everyone didn't know which they wanted to do more—hug him or let him have it— for that one!

Duran Duran's stay in New York needed no extra stimulation. While in the midst of their two Garden concerts, the band was whisked through days of worldwide press activities, including a photographic session with fashion king Francesco Scavullo, in which he did for Duran Duran what he does every month on those glamorous *Cosmo* covers. There was also a press conference for the group on March 21, the morning before their second New York show. With the exception of Simon, whose throat had been acting up, causing him to rest at the hotel, four tired band members turned up to face an army of reporters—some friends, some definitely not.

The gathering was held at the Greene Street Cafe, in the heart of the trendy Soho neighborhood. At that hour, the area normally is quiet—it's crammed full of artists and assorted "night people"—but here, pandemonium ruled. About a dozen fans waited hours in the cold, rainy street to catch a glimpse of Nick, Andy, John, and Roger, while inside photographers fell atop one another to gain a decent vantage point. After being given free reign to snap away for a while, the shutterbugs had to give way to a roomful of enterprising journalists, who represented every conceivable publication from *16 Magazine* to the *Wall Street Journal*, and came from all over the United States, England, Australia and Japan. Naturally, with that kind of diversity, the questions covered every conceivable topic, but most of them centered on how Duran Duran felt about their phenomenal success. Pretty good, was the unanimous response. Whenever the questioning turned to the band's so-called escapist attitude, tension did show itself. But by this point, the group had learned how to avoid letting hecklers get under their skin. Every popular artist must come to terms sooner or later with the fact that certain people will resent their popularity, and Duran Duran were no exception. As one open-minded reporter summed it up, "The tastes of the young are seldom appreciated."

When the press conference ended, an hour or so later, the four band members had their first opportunity to see the video of what would become their next single, "The Reflex." Shot at their Toronto concert earlier in the tour, the video was an abrupt departure from the exotic locations Duran Duran had relied upon before. This was almost straight concert footage, with a few bits of animation used for enhancement. Everyone was delighted with the result, including Roger, who deadpanned "Rubbish!" for benefit of the journalists. To the band, this raw, exciting video seemed right in line with the song's strong funk orientation.

The single mix of "The Reflex" was a dream come true for the band, who enlisted one of their heroes, Nile Rodgers of Chic, to supervise the sessions. Rodgers had been hired to work on the song for just two days, but he became so involved in it that he put in nine days, charing the same fee. The group were so thrilled with the result that, according to Andy, they were forced to defy Capitol Records, who were unsure that Duran Duran fans would accept such a highly rhythmic track. Horrified by the label's suggestion to instead release "Save a Prayer" from the almost two-year-old *Rio*, the band stuck to their guns—and of course, it was worth it. Released in the U.S. on April 6 and in Britain ten days later, "The Reflex" sent Duran Duran right back to the top of the charts, widening their audience even more to include some hardcore dance buffs.

If possible, the second Madison Square Garden concert was even more frenetic than the first, because this show was being broadcast to radio stations all over the U.S.A. By way of greeting their nationwide listeners, who numbered in the millions, Simon yelled out, "We're not just saying hello to you in New York; we're going out on a live broadcast to the whole of bleedin' America!" The crowd inside the Garden screamed out their approval, and the band delivered a show that surpassed expectations. An unexpected highlight was when Chic's Nile Rodgers and Tony Thompson joined Duran Duran onstage, and extended the final encore of "Girls on Film" into a twenty-minute jam session.

What a night—one which the group never wanted to end . . . so it didn't. Backstage, Simon and Clare happily meandered around, the four fathers present toasted their sons' accomplishment over some brews, and Andy and Nick got some advice about buying real estate in Manhattan from a man who should know—Andy Warhol. Later, Nick and his small entourage of girlfriend, bodyguard, and chums hung out at the trendy club called Limelight, then cruised through Manhattan until the sun rose. "That's the best sky I've seen for years," Rhodes said with quiet awe, winding back the limo's sunroof to take it all in. This was the kind of satisfaction no amount of money or adulation could buy.

Before the group left the New York area, they had one more surprise up their sleeves. Since Coca Cola, their sponsor, was also sponsoring the summer Olympics, a contest was conducted by the corporation and radio station Z-100 to see which city school could raise the most money for America's Olympic teams. The winners, Mark Twain Junior High School in Brooklyn, were treated to a very special prize—a visit by all of Duran Duran! As the thousand students cheered and screamed, the band gamely spoke to the teenagers, realizing that almost everything they said was drowned out by squeals. But it didn't matter, everyone agreed. The teachers protected their fragile eardrums with cotton, while the fans made their heroes feel very, very welcome.

All good times must finally end, and Duran Duran completed their wildly successful U.S. tour in California. Nick attended a fashion show, in which Julie Anne was modeling; that brought out photographers and fans in droves, forcing the couple to escape through a freight elevator. After their Los Angeles concerts, the group was thrown a party at Spago, a famous West Coast eatery. Among the many well-known faces who turned up to celebrate with the band were "Knots Landing's" Lisa Hartman and her boyfriend, Kiss guitarist Paul Stanley—who had seen his own share of fan mania a few years earlier.

They were ready to go home. The year 1984 had brought Duran Duran to the greatest numbers of people the group had ever played before. However, while delighted, everyone was also exhausted and just plain homesick. Andy missed Tracey terribly, and didn't intend to be away from her a moment longer than necessary. Nick admitted that he would have gone totally bananas without constant phone calls back to England. "I can't bear not knowing what's going on," he revealed. John returned to his newly purchased home that had nothing in it but a bed and a television set. "I might have a big bank balance but I've never had the time to enjoy the spoils of war; I've never had time to buy anything," he lamented. Only Simon, who had become much more physical as a result of such a lengthy tour, felt able to continue at its killing pace.

"I can't get used to the fact that I'm not playing a gig tonight," he confided, less than two weeks after the U.S. dates ended. "It's difficult for me to wind down; being on tour is just about the best form of physical exercise I know. I don't get tired, and when I'm off the road I don't know what to do with myself. I feel that I want to go out and start a revolution or something," Le Bon blurted, then immediately came down on himself for sounding so "pretentious."

It took a bit of doing before Duran Duran felt comfortable being home again. Their reputation as jet setters around America and the world got the band challenged by those who felt upset that they had ever left England. Trying to assure their British fans that this was, indeed, their home, Duran Duran settled in as best they could and devoted themselves to domestic matters. When "The Reflex" sailed onto the best-seller lists, the group appeared on "Top of the Pops," England's long-running countdown show. For too often, Duran Duran videos had substituted for the band, and the live appearance scored needed points. Simon, whose athletic presentation on the road led to knee injuries and a pulled tendon in one ankle, nonetheless did a guest spot on a Newcastle-based TV show, "Razzmatazz," before taking himself off to the doctor. Anyone coming in contact with the band could soon see that, despite their fame and wealth, when at home, Duran Duran were desperately trying to find some kind of normality in their lives.

"We're in a very pressurized situation," John conceded to *No. 1* magazine. "Being screamed at every night for six months, having your adrenalin and your ego pushed to the limit, makes it hard to go home. . . . Perhaps last year that arrogant pop star voice could have taken over, perhaps it even came close. But it didn't."

So as not to let those destructive influences come near, Duran Duran did at last force themselves to reduce their work schedule, postponing the release of the next studio album until early 1985. Instead, they expanded their involvement with Nile Rodgers, writing and recording a new single with his participation. That song is the only studio track on the band's latest album, an in-concert recording released in October. Completing the package is a full-length concert video cassette of the band, out at the same time. Before the year is over, though, Duran Duran will have begun the writing for a new album's worth of songs, and then, invariably, set back out on the road.

Meanwhile, both Nick and Simon have expressed interest in film work—Rhodes behind the camera and Le Bon in front of the lens. Simon has received so many offers for acting roles, ranging from a British cavalryman to the expected rock star scripts, that he may soon sign with a major agency for acting representation.

Thinking back of those first bone-chilling weeks working together, traveling throughout Britain in a beat up van, Duran Duran must find it hard to fully understand just how far they've come. Yet, believe it or not, their thoughts tend to settle onto how far they still have to go. Said Roger, "One day it'd be nice *not* to worry that if the next album isn't quite up to scratch, we could disappear without a trace." Millions of fans around the world could reassure Taylor and his mates that such a fate is hardly likely to be the case, but it's the band themselves who must eventually come to know that the respect they have earned by hard work and a positive attitude is theirs to keep, and they will be the only ones who could ever take it away.

APPENDIXES

DURAN DEVOTIONS: FAVORITES FROM DELICACIES TO DANCE CLUBS!

Simon Le Bon

Music: David Bowie, Thompson Twins, Stray Cats, Big Country, Doors, Rolling Stones, Chopin

Books: *The Magus*, *Our Man in Havana*, *Gormenghast* trilogy, anything from science fiction to Shakespeare.

Sports: Sailing, fencing

Hobbies: reading, watching TV and videos, shopping, going to films, writing, drawing, traveling

Food & Drink: tea, lemonade, chocolates, good wine, Indian food

Magazine: *Interview*

TV: "The Munsters"

Films: *ET*, *Diva*

Actors: Dirk Bogarde, Claudia Cardinale

Ideal Home: Seventy-foot yacht

Nick Rhodes

Music: Frank Sinatra, David Bowie, Roxy Music, Grace Jones, Eno, Yellow Magic Orchestra, Talking Heads, Donna Summer

Book: *From A to B and Back Again*, by Andy Warhol
Hobbies: photography, chess, Scrabble, board games, record producing, sleeping, collecting hats
Food & Drink: strawberries, champagne, Dover sole, Russian vodka, steak, Remy Martin, broccoli, potatoes, peas, carrots, the food in Australia!
Pet: Sebastian, a black cat
American TV shows: "The Munsters," "Family Feud"
Art: 1930s art deco, Andy Warhol, Patrick Nagel, Malcolm Garrett, Kandinsky, Roy Lichtenstein
Important Influence: *Ziggy Stardust & the Spiders From Mars*—David Bowie

Andy Taylor

Music: Bruce Springsteen, Sheena Easton, jazz, George Benson, Beatles, Rolling Stones, Clash, film soundtracks, Talking Heads, Mick Ronson, Diana Ross
Sports: horseback riding, tennis, water skiing, watching soccer
Food & Drink: potato chips, pasta, chicken, shellfish, milk, tea, big English lunches
TV: "The Young and the Restless," "Monty Python," "Star Trek," "Dallas"
Love Objects: wife, Tracey; children; lots of guitars
Animals: dogs, horses, parrots, lambs
Book: *Up the Organization*

John Taylor

Music: Roxy Music, Eurythmics, David Bowie, Chic, Abba, Japan, Rick James, Yellow Magic Orchestra, Johnny Thunders, New York Dolls, classical music
Food & Drink: his mother's cheese sandwiches, Thornton's chocolates, Galaxy bars, Big Macs,

DID YOU KNOW...? ONE HUNDRED SEMI-SECRETS

1. When he travels on the road, Simon carries tapes of new groups, plus old favorites including the Doors, Rolling Stones, David Bowie, and Talking Heads.
2. John owns a gold Aston Martin DB5 but rarely has time to drive it.
3. Simon's nickname from the rest of the group is "Charlie." An earlier nickname he had in London was "Muscles."
4. Andy and Tracey's wedding had been postponed three times before they finally tied the knot.
5. Roger hates English weather, particularly the winter!
6. Nick and Simon were asked to write a song for Marianne Faithfull, but didn't have the time.
7. John would love to appear in a show like "Dynasty," playing one of Joan Collins' lovers!
8. When Andy's not touring, he and Tracey get up around five or six A.M. to see their animals.
9. Simon used to physically shake during performances, he was so scared!
10. Roger's nickname is Froggy Barnacle, given to him by John because he snorkels.

11. Nick envies the fact that Roger's hair never goes out of place like his own does.

12. Simon can play the piano, marimba, Jew's harp, sax, flute, vibraphone, and violin.

13. The weirdest present the group ever received was a box of sand.

14. Simon was almost done in when a light fell into the pool he was swimming in, but some anonymous benefactor pulled it away just in time.

15. Andy wore an enormous brown beret while the band worked in Australia.

16. Simon sometimes signs autographs Simon Le Slob or Simon Le Bombe!

17. John dyed his bangs lilac in Australia, but the hot sun turned them bright pink!

18. Roger turns red when he gets embarrassed.

19. When the group opened for Hazel O'Connor, they were often spit on by the punky crowd.

20. Simon used to tell people that this parents were Russian refugees, because he thought his real life was too boring.

21. Roger almost became a postman before he joined the band.

22. Simon is 6′2″ tall.

23. Roger is 5′10½″ tall.

24. Nick is 5′9″ tall.

25. Andy is 5′7″ tall.

26. John is 6′1″ tall.

27. John's nicknames are "JT" and "Trigger."

28. Duran Duran's fan club receives over two thousand letters each week!

29. Over twenty people work for the band all year round, not counting their road crew.

30. Simon went back to Sri Lanka by himself for a holiday in 1983.

31. One of John's hobbies is collecting Japanese magazines.

32. When Duran Duran's charity concert in Birming-

ham lost money, the group chipped in $7,500 out of their pockets.

33. Some fans have spent as much as $5,000 to pursue the group around the world!

34. Roger's unflappable calmness helps keep tempers from flaring during any tiffs.

35. Nick says he's proud of the Greenham Common women's peace movement in England.

36. Andy and Tracey live in a fifteenth-century cottage in Shropshire.

37. Andy bought a restaurant in Newcastle and called it "Rio."

38. While working in Sydney, the band were guests at the Australian Film Institute Awards.

39. Simon's family is descended from the Huguenots, and has its own coat of arms.

40. John's first car was a VW Golf (Rabbit to us Yanks).

41. Andy and Tracey have a horse named Bobby.

42. Before achieving their first U.S. Top 40 hit, Duran Duran already had six foreign hit singles.

43. As a child, Roger decorated his room with Beatles wallpaper.

44. Ten thousand fans lined up to get two thousand tickets for Duran Duran's royal concert.

45. Nick has created a collection of his photographs called "Interference".

46. John is deeply hurt by negative articles about the band.

47. Duran Duran wish they could own a TV station!

48. Simon prefers dying his hair blond, rather than keeping it natural brown.

49. Nick has changed his hair color so often, he's often warned about it falling out!

50. The original U.S. *Duran Duran* album is now a hard-to-find collector's item.

51. The band often puts in sixteen-hour work days.

52. Posh English designer John Kaye is the group's current favorite.

53. Andy's brother-in-law often travels with Duran Duran as their hairdresser.

54. Andy has produced a local Birmingham group called the Bloomsbury Set.

55. John has to be in a very special mood to be persuaded onto a dance floor.

56. Simon would *not* appear nude in a film, even if he was asked!

57. When Duran Duran's video album was premiered at Studio 54, over eight thousand people showed up.

58. In Montserrat, Andy had to dispose of a huge spider which had climbed onto his wash.

59. John spent a day sailing off Montserrat despite hurricane warnings.

60. Duran Duran's British fans throw flowers, jewelry, and teddy bears at them.

61. Nick considers himself to be the most fashion-conscious of the band.

62. Roger once despaired of the group ever making it big in America.

63. Roger still wants to be in Duran Duran ten years from now!

64. "Girls on Film" is the only Duran Duran video that was banned.

65. Roger had hoped to visit the Australian outback but never had enough time.

66. Nick's next production project might be for a new band called Days at Sea.

67. Roger is an accomplished percussionist who plays congas and bells.

68. John luxuriates in a bed which measures 6 × 6 feet.

69. Duran Duran would love to make videos in China and Iceland!

70. During his punk years, Simon sometimes slept in Hyde Park.

71. It cost Duran Duran about $150,000 to do their second American tour.

72. Male Duran Duran fans who resemble the band often get asked for autographs—and sign them!

73. John got bitten by a wombat in Australia—fortunately, not badly.

74. When Simon put on a little weight, the group teased him by calling him "Lardo."

75. Andy and Tracey own a three-storey house in Wolverhampton along with his brother and one of hers.

76. Duran Duran's concerts attract lots of people in their twenties and thirties, not just teenagers.

77. Andy grew his hair so long last fall, he tied it in a pony tail.

78. Nick has never forgiven himself for doing a rush editing job on "Hold Back the Rain."

79. Nick is very involved with the technical side of recording.

80. Nick likes to stay up all night when he's in New York.

81. Nick runs up a huge phone bill calling home when he travels.

82. Roger wishes he could play drums like Chic's Tony Thompson.

83. Duran Duran love the way their name looks on album covers.

84. There are at least three bootleg Duran Duran concert LPs on the market.

85. While in a Japanese high-rise, the group was caught in an earthquake!

86. Duran Duran do talk about political issues, but don't believe in publicizing their views.

87. The band spent one thousand hours recording *Seven and the Ragged Tiger*.

88. Until they got too popular, the group used to explore towns where they were performing.

89. On their first trip to New York, Nick, John, and Roger ate Egg McMuffins at six A.M.

90. John Taylor regrets that the group became famous too late for him to date a "Charlie's Angel."
91. The band wishes they weren't always compared to someone—first Spandau Ballet, lately Culture Club.
92. Nick used to wash the family car for a few pence (about fifteen cents!) way back when.
93. If Duran Duran ever broke up, Nick would direct films.
94. Roger prefers watching exotic sunsets to watching TV.
95. John feels that Japan is the most underrated group of all time.
96. Simon is so forgetful, he misplaced half a dozen Walkmans in less than a year!
97. Roger is determined to keep his private life out of the newspapers.
98. Andy's nickname is Sniffer.
99. John's family had a fit when they first saw his dyed hair.
100. Nick is called Ringo, because he hates it!

SOME THINGS DURAN DURAN
HAS TOLD THE PRESS

—**If you ruled the world, how would you like to travel?**
John: By flying jacuzzi.

—**What are your bad habits?**
Andy: Biting my nails and I stay up too late. I also shout at the dog.

—**Who has a sense of humor to help the band through rough times?**
Roger: There are no humorists in this band. We're all miserable people! (Laughs)

—**When do you plan to undertake solo projects?**
John: When the band breaks up.
Andy: When we get a couple of days off.
Simon: I'll let you know that's not true!

—**What would you like to change about your looks?**
John: I wouldn't be so knock-kneed.

—**To what extent are you involved with your fan club activities?**
Simon: Obviously, we can't participate in those things while we're on tour, but we write things for the fan letters and we see a lot of the mail.

Nick: Especially the rude letters, the ones with the pictures of naked women!

—**Are you superstitious?**
Roger: No, I'm not superstitious at all. I walk under ladders all the time.

—**Will you make your next video in the Himalayas?**
Andy: Someone's trying to convince us to go there.
Nick: It's a vicious rumor.
John: Not if me and Nick have anything to do with it!

—**Do you respect your audience?**
Simon: Yes, I do very much and for a lot of different reasons as well. Because they've got the common sense to like decent music like ours, and for sticking by us in the face of great adversity.

—**How do you feel about the lifetime commitment of marriage?**
Simon: I believe that if you make big promises like that you should keep them.

—**Do you argue with one another?**
Nick: Actually, we get on very well. We have a good laugh together. Of course there are heated moments. I'd just be lying if I said that we get on like little angels all the time.

—**What was your first impression of the other band members?**
Roger: I thought John was very friendly, Nick was reserved, Andy was loud, and Simon overenthusiastic. It's still exactly the same.

—**Is it disconcerting having to play and not being able to see the people you're playing to?**
Andy: As long as they can see us, I think that's the

*important thing. They are paying the money to come
and see us. That's why we use the big video screen
above us.*

—**Do you have more female fans than male fans?**
Simon: I don't know; I've never counted them all up!

—**Would you ever write music specifically for a video?**
*Simon: No, it's not a good thing to do because, you
see, we're based in music, that's where our hearts
lie, and if we started concentrating on the visual
the songs would suffer, and I don't think it would
be a very credible thing to do.*

—**When you were first getting the band together, did
you feel that the original members weren't just right?**
*John: No, they actually felt that we were inadequate.
That's why they let.*

—**How do you feel about doing a duet with somebody?**
*Simon: Vocally? I'm not at that stage yet. I'd love to
work with Dolly Parton though; I think she's so
funny....She looks great, and has the most incredible bosom.*

—**Is it frightening to imagine your success ending?**
*Nick: No, I don't worry about things like that. If it
stops, it stops. You know we'd continue to do something else and come back again.*

—**Is one member of the band the most popular?**
*Simon: In England, there are very few bands in which
each member is recognized. But everybody knows
all of Duran Duran. We have five individual looks.
We all get stopped on the street, and we're very
proud of that.*

—**How much luggage do you take on the road?**

John: I've had to trim things down a bit—one regular suitcase, one suit bag, and one quite large carry-on case. But we have wardrobes that go with the group. All you need is the essential—as long as you've got your toothbrush, you can always get by.

—**Would you ever see a psychoanalyst?**

Simon: No. I'd rather find out about myself through myself. To start with, I'm very happy with myself; I don't think there's anything wrong with me. It also seems very vain to pay someone else to talk about you.

—**What happens to the presents that are tossed onstage?**

Nick: Everything that's labeled goes to the person in question. Otherwise, they go to whoever fancies them. Nothing is thrown away. I've got loads of scarves. I think almost every scarf I own has been thrown onstage.

—**Do you ever wonder why so many girls like you?**

John: I'm not falsely modest to sit and wonder about it, but at the same time, I think if I was to get engaged tomorrow, publicly, it'd be Roger that would start to get the attention. I don't really take that much notice of it. In fact, I probably get more embarrassed about it.

—**Why does Boy George get away with wearing makeup and you don't?**

Nick: Because we didn't wear such gaudy colors as he.

—**Apart from their music how have the Beatles influenced the Pop scene?**

Roger: The Beatles proved you could be musicians and media favorites by showing people you have a sense of humor.

—**What is most satisfying to you?**

Simon: *Being onstage. It's a really big challenge; it's really dangerous in a way. Every night before I go on, I have a kind of trauma about whether I can do it tonight.*

—**Would you ever consider dating a fan?**

Nick: *Yes. I've not only considered it; I've done it. I like girls with a great sense of humor and a really good personality.*

U.S. DISCOGRAPHY

Singles

6/81: Planet Earth/To the Shore
9/81: Girls on Film/Faster Than Light
6/82: Hungry Like the Wolf/Careless Memories
10/82: Rio/Hold Back the Rain
12/82: Hungry Like the Wolf (remix)/Hungry (night version)
3/83: Rio (remix)/Hold Back the Rain
5/83: Is There Something I Should Know?/Careless Memories
10/83: Union of the Snake/Secret Oktober
1/84: New Moon on Monday/Tiger Tiger
4/84: The Reflex/New Religion
9/84: new single

Albums

6/81: Duran Duran (now deleted)
5/82: Rio
9/82: Carnival mini-LP (now deleted)
4/83: Duran Duran (same as first album, except with remixed tracks + "Is There Something I Should Know?")
11/83: Seven and the Ragged Tiger
10/84: new live album

144

Album Tracks

Duran Duran

Planet Earth
Girls on Film
Is There Anyone Out There
Careless Memories
(Waiting For the) Night Boat
Sound of Thunder
Friends of Mine
Tel Aviv

Rio

Rio
My Own Way
Lonely in Your Nightmare
Hungry Like The Wolf
Hold Back the Rain
New Religion
Last Chance on the Stairway
Save a Prayer
The Chauffeur

Mini-LP (remixed versions)

Hungry Like the Wolf
Girls on Film
Hold Back the Rain
My Own Way

Duran Duran (1983 version)

same as first album, except with remixed tracks +
"Is There Something I Should Know?"

Seven and the Ragged Tiger

The Reflex
New Moon on Monday
(I'm Looking For) Cracks in the Pavement
I Take the Dice
Of Crime and Passion
Union of the Snake
Shadows on Your Side
Tiger Tiger
The Seventh Stranger

VIDEOGRAPHY

3/83: Video Album: Planet Earth, Careless Memories, Girls on Film, My Own Way, Hungry Like the Wolf, Save a Prayer, Rio, Lonely in Your Nightmare, Night Boat, The Chauffeur, Is There Something I Should Know?
4/83: Sony Video 45: Hungry Like the Wolf/Girls on Film
Promotional videos: 9/83: Union of the Snake
2/84: New Moon on Monday
5/84: The Reflex
10/84: In concert Video Album

FAN CLUB INFORMATION

Duran Duran Club
273 Broad Street
Birmingham B1 2DS, England

ABOUT THE AUTHOR

*T*oby Goldstein has been a critical observer of the rock music and entertainment scene since 1971, and a rock'n'roll fan for a good many years before that. She has written for many U.S. and international publications and, for three years, broadcast New York music news as a radio correspondent over CBC (Canada) and BBC Radio One (UK). Currently feature editor of *Soap Opera Digest*, Ms. Goldstein remains an active contributing editor to the long-lived rock magazines *Creem* and *Hit Parader*. She originally interviewed Duran Duran for a *Creem* profile in 1982.